JE NE SAIS QUOI

DEVOREAUX WALTON

**MOUNTAIN ARBOR
PRESS**
Alpharetta, GA

Copyright © 2019 by Devoreaux Walton. All rights reserved. Without limiting the rights under copyrights reserved above, no part of this publication may be reproduced, stored in or introduced into a retrieval system, or transmitted, in any form or by any means (electronic, mechanical, photocopying, scanning, video presentation, audio recording, or otherwise), without the prior written permission from the author of this book.

Library of Congress Control Number: 2019901831
ISBN-13: 978-1-63183-567-4

10 9 8 7 6 5 4 3 2 1   0 4 2 3 1 9

For additional information about the author, to book a signing event, or for information on acquiring written permission in the case of brief quotations embodied in critical articles, interviews and reviews, please visit www.DevoreauxWalton.com.

Cover design and layout by Daymond E. Lavine of Moksha Media, moksha-media.com.

To any woman who has ever dared to keep her heels, head, and standards high.

Your light shines in this world of darkness.

Contents

Foreword v

Introduction 1

Part 1: Confidence 9
   Chapter 1: Mastering Your Mindset 11
   Chapter 2: Graceful Self-Discovery 38
   Chapter 3: Choosing Happiness 66

Part 2: Care 83
   Chapter 4: Personal Style 85
   Chapter 5: Beauty Routine 122
   Chapter 6: Healthy Habits 149

Part 3: Charm 171
   Chapter 7: Compelling Character 173
   Chapter 8: Polished Presence 205
   Chapter 9: Social Graces 221

Part 4: Competence 231
   Chapter 10: Standard of Excellence 233
   Chapter 11: Career Success 255

Part 5: Composure 291
   Chapter 12: Captivating Communication 293
   Chapter 13: Overcoming Difficulty 321

Part 6: Class 343
   Chapter 14: Everyday Elegance 345

The Journey of Je Ne Sais Quoi 354

Acknowledgments 356

About the Author 358

Foreword

In a world where etiquette and manners seem to have gone extinct, Devoreaux Walton's voice is sorely needed. Through her coaching company and YouTube channel, The Modern Lady, Devoreaux reaches out to women all around the world sharing her timeless and much needed lessons on elegance and poise.

Devoreaux asked me to write the foreword of this lovely book because we both believe in the powerful message that anyone can have class and poise. These are not qualities you buy. They aren't even qualities you are born with. You must work on them every day and we are all works in progress.

Je Ne Sais Quoi is full of timeless wisdom that could propel the upcoming generation to greatness. While most people with their faces firmly fixed on their smartphones, allow the world to pass them by, you will be encouraged through this book to shine brighter than the screens those people are fixated upon.

Devoreaux's tips on style, grooming, etiquette, and attitude will take you very far in life. Having poise is a rare attribute. Once you practice that je ne sais quoi, you will stand out from the crowd and be amazed at the doors that will open for you.

As Devoreaux writes, "This is your defining moment. There is no better time than right now to start uncovering your je ne sais quoi." To that wonderful call-to-action, I say, let the defining moment begin.

Jennifer L. Scott
New York Times Bestselling Author,
Lessons from Madame Chic

Introduction

Have you ever said to yourself: "I need to get my life together!?" I have. I said it so many times that I lost count. After several years of being frustrated with every area of my life – from my lack of a polished wardrobe, to my sluggish demeanor from eating excessive junk food, to working a job I couldn't stand, to being gauche in social settings – I was tired of being stuck in a rut. I wanted to change, and more importantly, I was ready to change.

In an effort to give my entire life a makeover, I went on a journey to discover, define, and develop the confident, classy, charismatic woman I always wanted to be. I reviewed the impact of faith, energy, and mindset to reinvent myself. I read books by Emily Post. I researched my sheroes, Jacqueline Kennedy and Michelle Obama. I studied and applied elegant style and lifestyle principles to my life. And I experienced an amazing transformation. I greeted each day with joy in my heart. I took delight in conversations with eloquence. I stood tall in any room with grace. I was living with je ne sais quoi. And now, I want to empower you to live with je ne sais quoi, too.

I define je ne sais quoi as your source of feminine power. It's the alluring, elegant, captivating, enchanting essence of who you are, demonstrated through how you live. The appealing nature of your mindset, presence, and wardrobe are physical manifestations of your je ne sais quoi.

I believe that every woman has the potential to uncover and unleash her je ne sais quoi; it's just a matter of redefining your life to lead with grace and dignity. Living with je ne sais quoi allows you to let class, character, and confidence take the front seat to drive the car in your life. On each day and for every decision you make, you have the beautiful opportunity to make a choice. You choose what you think, say, do, and wear, which creates your lifestyle.

One theme you will find in this book is the intersection of making empowering choices and being intentional in how you live. A woman with je ne sais quoi is refined, sophisticated, and kind, which requires making daily choices to reinforce her compellingly elegant manner. You always have the option to be charming, gracious, and tasteful in how you carry yourself, or to be nonchalant, insensitive, and rude. This book will explore how you can create new habits to consistently choose an elegant life, with je ne sais quoi.

Just like any new habit, like learning how to speak French fluently, you will become stronger in your new skillset the more often you use the skills themselves. Each day is a blessing. You have the opportunity to choose je ne sais quoi in every thought you ponder; word you speak; garment you wear; and action you take. Each time you decide to live with je ne sais quoi, you are reinforcing your new elegant life habits. Over time, the practice will become second nature. When you no longer have to choose consciously to live with je ne sais quoi, you will instinctively choose elegant thoughts, words, clothing, and actions.

You were not put on this Earth for mediocrity, to barely get by each day, feeling empty and unsatisfied. You are here for a divine purpose, and it's to maximize your potential and truly prosper. Discovering je ne sais quoi will help you to elevate your life by sprinkling delight and satisfaction over your mindset, appearance, relationships, and presence. Once you enhance your life with je ne sais quoi, you may even surprise yourself by how amazing you feel, look, and live.

Upon discovering your je ne sais quoi, you will never be the same. You become a more refined and radiant version of yourself. You will feel a sense of strength, poise, and charm in what you think, say, do and wear. And those around you will feel it, too. They will be both inspired and impressed by you, whether they share their praise or not. Your personal and professional success will lead you to live your best life.

This is your defining moment. There is no better time than right now to start uncovering your je ne sais quoi. If you can relate to feeling stuck in a rut like I did, in any area of your life – your self-talk, wardrobe, presence, relationships, or career – then I encourage you to read this book and apply the elegant principles you'll learn, so that you can take yourself and your life to the next level. You deserve to embrace and enjoy your life without negativity, unfulfillment, or discontent. Now is your time to step out of the shadows and turn up your light. Leave the past behind you, and look forward toward your bold, bright, elegant future. One quote I wrote down and reviewed daily during my journey to discover je ne sais quoi is from Ella Fitzgerald: "It isn't where you came from, it's where you're going that counts."

It's no secret that today we live in a world of darkness. Every time you turn on the news, you see a negative report. The culture we live in encourages selfishness, hatred, and impatience. People are quick to criticize and slow to compliment. Women are taught from the media (television, magazines, and movies) to flaunt themselves by wearing less clothing, showing every curve they have, piling on pounds of makeup, and 'fixing' their 'trouble areas' with surgery, injections, and pills.

Although this is the world that we live in, it doesn't have to define *your* world. It is my hope that this book's inspiration, encouragement, and guidance will help you to redefine your own world with elegance. This book serves to illuminate your light in this dark world. I hope that everything I have learned (and continue to learn) about living with elegance helps to change your life for the better.

I believe that an elegant life is an empowered life. It's about confidence over conceit. It's about gracefulness over aggressiveness. It's about sophistication over sloppiness. Living with je ne sais quoi is about being thoughtful in applying intention to who you are and how you live. I trust that within these pages you will be encouraged to discover the lady within and step into your full power, led by your feminine greatness to live out every day with je ne sais quoi.

As you read this book and explore who you are and who you want to be as an elegant woman, I recommend you bring a journal or notebook along with you for the excursion. You'll find sections with Actionable Advice for you to complete exercises helping you to define your charming nature. You'll also review Chic Life Secrets with brief reminders for living with elegance. This book is your companion to creating the elegant life you've always dreamed of.

Ready to elevate yourself with je ne sais quoi? Let's embark on this journey together. And the endeavor begins . . .

May your days be full of confidence, class, and charisma

PART 1
CONFIDENCE

CHAPTER 1

MASTERING YOUR MINDSET

You are more powerful than you know; you are beautiful just as you are.

Melissa Etheridge

The foundation of a life with je ne sais quoi starts from within. The thoughts you carry consistently create your energy, which is the powerful mental capacity that creates your vibration or overall state of being. As you very well know, we are all our harshest critics, but I urge you to take the idea a bit further and consider this: when it comes to self-talk, you have two inner critics. Just like a cartoon movie you likely watched as a child with an angel on one shoulder and a devil on the other shoulder, you too, have not one but two inner critics. Which of the two critics do you listen to more often? Which one more often guides your thoughts, actions, and interactions?

The truth is, every thought within your mind is born from your self-talk. What you tell yourself is a powerful thing because it inspires what you believe. And more importantly, the way you think is driven by the self-talk you consciously and unconsciously meditate on.

As a first step to mastering your mindset, it's helpful to take notice of which critic you hear speaking within you when your self-talk ignites. Pleasant, uplifting, optimistic thoughts are from your positive conscience – the inner critic that aims to be righteous in the world. Fearful, discouraging, pessimistic thoughts are from your negative conscience – the inner critic that aims to wreak havoc in the world. Your positive conscience is selfless while your negative conscience is selfish. As you go about your day, from home to work to play dates to happy hour to date nights, you'll hear self-talk constantly. Identifying which inner critic is speaking will help you to navigate whether or not you should turn the volume up or turn the volume off on that inside voice.

Actionable Advice

As you get to know your inner critics, name both your positive and negative conscience to give each of the voices a persona.

Examples for your positive conscience include The Queen, Boss Lady, and Wonder Woman.

Examples for your negative conscience include Doubting Tina, Damsel in Distress, and Cruella de Vil.

Once you brainstorm and decide on the creative, cute names for your inner critics, write them down in your journal.

My positive conscience is _____.

My negative conscience is _____.

* * * * *

JE NE SAIS QUOI

Consider this: you're getting dressed for a blind date that your best friend arranged. You've been out of the dating game for a year and are feeling a bit uneasy about it, but you decide to go, nonetheless. As you spray Chanel N°5 on each wrist, you look in the mirror and hear your inner critic say, "This is useless, he's going to be just like the last guy, obnoxious and annoying. Why even bother dating, I'm going to be single forever!" Which of the two inner critics do you think inspired that thought? If you guessed your negative conscience, you're right! Upon hearing your negative conscience, you can acknowledge her (name and all!) and put her in her rightful place, which is under your authority and control. That voice deserves to be turned down to make room for your positive conscience to speak up. The voice that says, "I'm going to have fun tonight, meeting someone new that Chelsea wants me to meet. I trust my best friend. She wouldn't connect me with anyone less than a gentleman!"

Your two inner critics will always have something to say about every situation, person and outcome, and it's your job to lead with your positive conscience instead of your negative conscience. Your life with je ne sais quoi is supported by your positive conscience, with your negative conscience kept in check. Both consciences will compete for your attention (they are hungry for it!), but you can choose which of the two that you will lean on for guiding your thoughts and actions. Allowing your positive conscience to create your energy leads to living with a pleasant, confident vibration, or state of being.

THE LAW OF ATTRACTION

I am going to let you in on a secret: your vibration influences your outcomes. This is the simple Law of Attraction at play, the concept that your thoughts manifest your ideas into existence. Once you realize the immense power that your mindset has, you can begin to master it. When you have a thought, you are either supporting or opposing the outcome you want in life. In both small and major ways, your thoughts become your reality. It may surprise or even shock you when you start thinking of things only to later experience exactly what you thought about, which is why selecting which of your two inner critics you listen to is so important. Your conscience guides your thoughts, which guide your actions and interactions. The dreams, hopes, fears, and insecurities you carry in your heart will be reinforced with the self-talk from your conscience, which drives what you think, say, and do with others.

Let's explore how the Law of Attraction can apply to an everyday occurrence. For example, upon finding the perfect pair of Manolo Blahnik pumps online, you find that your size is unavailable, so you call a local store to see if they have a size 7 in stock. As you wait on hold, you allow your positive conscience to take charge. Your self-talk thoughts are: "I'm sure they have a size 7, it's probably just in the back, so I'll be patient while they find my pair. These shoes are meant just for me!" Within moments of sending positive energy and vibrations to the universe, the store manager picks up the phone and excitedly shares that they have located the last pair in a 7, and they will hold the beautiful heels for you at the cashier until you pick them up. See how the law of attraction can work in your favor?

Now, if you had let your negative conscience take charge with thoughts like, "I guess I missed out since they don't have my size. The whole world is just against me," you may have been so mired in frustration and doubt from discovering that the website didn't have your size that you would not have even considered calling the store and inquiring about a size 7 at a nearby location! You would have missed out on the perfect pair of pumps.

In any given situation, you want a specific outcome. Allowing your positive conscience to dominate your self-talk will help you to fortify your energy and vibration, sprinkling seeds of positivity in the universe. The positive influence will reinforce the outcome that you want (like finding your size in a gorgeous pair of pumps) and impact the results you experience. As you strive for a goal or objective, meditating on positivity will help you to achieve the desires of your heart.

BUT FIRST, GRATITUDE

Throughout life, you will have winning moments – the wonderful, unexpected little blessings that happen when you least expect them. When ordering a pumpkin spice latte and the barista gives you a croissant for free, that is a winning moment. When getting compliments from co-workers on your new tweed blazer, that is a winning moment. When sitting on the porch in the evening with your family watching the sunset, that is a winning moment.

An exhilarating, successful, delightful life is available to you – to unlock the door, you will need to fortify your mindset with gratitude. It's important to recognize and honor the winning moments that you have each day to develop a gracious heart. These celebrations elevate the importance of every positive moment you experience. When you embrace winning moments, more of them will begin to happen! A more positive life is a more prosperous life. Think of good things, and good things will become your constant reality.

You can and will experience the abundance of everything life has to offer if your mindset allows you to be open to receiving it. Your mindset about resources (time, money, and opportunities) typically falls into one of two categories – an abundance mindset or a scarcity mindset. Abundance means there is more than enough of a resource. Imagine an open bar at a cocktail party: there is no shortage of prosecco all evening long! An abundance mindset utilizes the power of positivity and is full of beliefs and ideas that there are more than enough resources in this world for all to enjoy. Scarcity means there is a limited amount of a resource. Imagine a cocktail party with a one drink maximum: you better cherish that glass of prosecco because it's the only one you'll have for the night! A scarcity mindset utilizes the power of negativity and is full of beliefs and ideas that there are not enough resources for all of us to enjoy our fair share.

Having an abundance mindset versus a scarcity mindset can influence your outlook and actions in a given situation. Your inner critics have a lot to say about these types of mindsets. Your positive conscience will automatically revert to an abundance mindset while your negative conscience will automatically revert to a scarcity mindset.

If you just learned about free tickets available for the newest opera production in town from a radio commercial, your abundance mindset will encourage you to share the good news with everyone you know interested in live theater performances. Your scarcity mindset, on the other hand, will encourage you to keep the good news to yourself – only telling your family and friends *after* you've secured tickets for yourself first.

A life with je ne sais quoi relies on an abundance mindset. Instead of hoarding the treasures and talents that you have in life, you can freely share them with others and selflessly have the mentality to pay it forward. The talents and skills you have are a gift from God and are meant to be a blessing not just for yourself, but for everyone around you. There is more than enough money, happiness, and opportunity in this world for everyone to attain their fair share of success. Be open to teaching, encouraging, and helping others when you can – that is one of the many reasons we are all here in this world together.

Gratitude reinforces abundance because when you focus on counting the blessings you have; your mindset will start to broaden its horizon. You will wake up to realize the fact that you are fortunate and favored. Cultivating a mindset focused on gratitude is one of the many daily habits of a life with je ne sais quoi. To create an elegant mind, you can develop a pattern of being thankful for everything in your life, both big and small.

Actionable Advice

How you start the day is how you finish.

As such, you can take small but definite steps every day to reinforce your gratitude recognition and unlock the power of your elegant mindset. Be thankful for your winning moments as well as the many blessings you have like: your family, friends, loved ones, talents, income, home, and belongings.

Spend five to ten minutes every morning in your journal writing everything that comes to mind that you are grateful for. This practice of Gratitude Journaling will help you to fast-track your day with an elegant mindset. Throughout your day, it will be easier to carry yourself with elegance because of this graceful morning ritual.

Every single day, you have an endless number of things to be grateful for. This morning routine will help you to be aware and acknowledge your fortunate circumstances instead of taking them for granted. Give yourself grace as you view your life with this new pair of rose-colored gratitude glasses. If you list the same 15 things in your journal each day in your morning routine, that is okay. You can never be too grateful for the blessings in your life. Writing them down daily is a beautiful reminder to your mind, body, and soul of how fortunate you are.

And your day ahead is sure to be filled with elegance, based on the focus you place on gratitude. This morning routine is your 'me time' to power up your mindset as you prepare for the day. Think of it this way: you brush your hair to have it looking its best before you leave home, right? This gratitude habit will help your mindset to be at its best before you leave home, too.

A life with je ne sais quoi doesn't occasionally include gratitude, it consistently does. Spending a few minutes every day (not just on the days you feel like it) to complete this exercise will help you to thrive with elegance. Consistency is key to both mastering and maintaining your mindset.

*****

A daily morning routine focused on gratitude helps to channel your attention on positivity rather than negativity, making it easier to live with optimism. When you spend the first few moments of your day counting your blessings, it will be easier to apply optimism to what you experience. The more frequently you focus on pleasantness, the more pleasantness you will find. If you happen to find living with optimism a challenge, you can sprinkle extra doses of gratitude throughout your day instead of waiting for your morning 'me time' to uncover things to be thankful for. Instead of complaining about a person or situation, find something within it to praise. The only way to drive out darkness is to turn up the light. Brighten your life with gratitude and search for the silver lining when circumstances end up less than what you had hoped for.

LIVING WITH OPTIMISM

An elegant mindset is a positive mindset. Your ability to look for the good in people, places, and things will serve you well in a life with je ne sais quoi. Optimism is powerful. When you live with hope in your heart, you know that there is nothing you can't conquer. Challenges will come, but you can overcome them. Difficulties may arise, but you can rise above them. As you're learning how to master your mindset, you will likely have to change how you think. When faced with a less-than-desirable circumstance, you will have to wake up your positive conscience and turn up her volume. She will lead you to discover the sunshine after the rain.

There is a beautiful concept called the silver lining, and this is the perfect notion to make sure you understand what it is, so you and your positive conscience can look for it. When something negative occurs in a situation, you can identify something pleasant or positive from what has happened despite how dark or dismal it may be. To find the silver lining, ask yourself this question: "What is the good in this situation?" in the heat of disappointment.

An optimistic mindset is the starting point to a life with poise, power, and je ne sais quoi.

For example, you and your husband are house hunting, and after four months of searching, you've found **the one**. It's a beautiful, open concept condo with a large walk-in closet (for all your handbags and shoes, of course!), located in the heart of downtown overlooking the skyline, and it's within your budget! After submitting your offer to the seller, you are outbid by someone with cash, and the picture-perfect condo is no longer on the market. Now you're back to square one, house hunting again. Despite your disappointment, consider the Elegant Mindset Question: "What is the good in this situation?" You found a place that checked off all the boxes on your list of must-haves for a new home, so you know that the condo of your dreams is available and exists. After reviewing this property, you are one step closer to finding your new home. You found a condo community that fits all your wants and needs, and perhaps another unit will be listed for sale soon.

Actionable Advice

Write down on a sticky note or 3′ x 5′ index card the Elegant Mindset Question: "What is the good in this situation?" and place it somewhere visible with easy access for viewing, perhaps on your desk at work or your bathroom mirror. This beautiful question is a reminder for you to revert to when faced with a setback or challenge. Your life will include disappointments, but how you deal with them makes all the difference in your je ne sais quoi lifestyle. Reviewing this question regularly is a lovely reminder for you to find the silver lining in the challenges that come your way.

* * * * *

You may have heard the famous phrase, "Life is like a box of chocolates, you never know what you're gonna get." Let's face it, your days will be full of highs and lows, celebrations and disappointments, but your ability to live with optimism allows you to carry yourself every day with elegance through the good and the not-so-good times. When a situation results in something other than what you had hoped for, ask yourself the Elegant Mindset Question: "What is the good in this situation?" and look for the silver lining, sifting through the troubles to find what is terrific about it.

CONQUERING FEAR & SELF-DOUBT

We all have some fear of uncertainty. When you aren't sure of the outcome from something you are working toward, those are the moments to take a deep breath and, as Susan Jeffers says, "Feel the fear and do it anyway."

Believe it or not, I think fear is a good thing. Fear is nervous energy that can be channeled to help you surpass your goals, dreams, and expectations. Fear is a sign that you are on the right track, doing something that stretches you outside your comfort zone, and pushing you to achieve greatness. Recognizing that fear is present in your thoughts is another wake-up call for your positive conscience. When you are fearful of pursuing something because you're uncertain of the outcome, it's time to turn up the volume of that inner voice that will encourage you to go for it. Apply for the job of your dreams, even if you don't think you are qualified. Take a chance on moving to a new city, even if you don't know anyone that lives there. Attend the charity gala to support your local non-profit, even if meeting new people over fine dining makes you weak at the knees.

Any time you have a thought centered on how you can't or shouldn't do something, those ideas are referred to as self-limiting beliefs. Your negative conscience tells them to you, and as such, they have no rightful place in your mind. When they start to creep up, you can dismiss the self-limiting beliefs by turning off the voice of your negative conscience and turning up the voice of your positive conscience. Instead of allowing self-limiting beliefs to swim around in your mind, be selective to allow only self-empowering beliefs to swim in your mind instead. Change every thought that starts with "I can't" to "I can" and from "I won't" to "I will." Let your positive conscience always lead the way.

As Tony Robbins once said, "Where focus goes, energy flows." He was right. In every encounter, focus on the most positive outcome possible – it's time to start shifting your thoughts to harness the power of your mindset for good outcomes, not bad ones. We tend to think of the worst-case scenario as a default; often, it's the go-to thought when you consider pursuing taking action toward your goals.

I'd like to challenge that thinking. When it comes to your plans for the future, instead of thinking to yourself, "What's the worst thing that could happen?" shift your thoughts to ask yourself, "What's the *best thing* that could happen?" I like to call this mindset motivator the Best-Case Scenario. A life with je ne sais quoi always errs on the side of hopefulness.

> *Worrying is a prayer for what you don't want to happen.*
>
> Robert Downey Jr.

Your mindset either fuels you with ambition and passion for your dreams or drowns you in fear that disconnects you from your dreams entirely. The direction your mindset will take you relies ultimately on the choices you make. I encourage you to choose to think of the best thing that can happen, not the worst.

With full confidence and a strong belief in yourself, the only question is not if you will accomplish your goals, but <u>when</u> you will accomplish your goals. Continue to focus on the good in people and situations until positive thinking becomes such a habit that it is second nature, and you are regularly thinking positively to live with optimism so that conquering fear and doubt becomes a breeze.

All too often, as women, we downplay and discount how amazing and talented we truly are. We think we aren't good enough, pretty enough, tall enough, slim enough, or smart enough. Those false thoughts can deter us from achieving or even pursuing goals and dreams, and those are the very thoughts that need to be turned off to allow room to turn on positive thoughts instead.

The reality is that we all have a superhero within. As a young girl, your mind swirled with limitless possibilities. You were invincible. You were unstoppable. But as you matured into an adult, reality set in and likely tainted your upbeat view of the world.

It is time to find that fearless spirit again and allow it to guide you. Let positivity prevail!

REIGNING OVER YOUR MINDSET

An elegant mindset is simple but not easy to attain. Truthfully, what is easy is automatically dwelling on negativity. It's comfortable and convenient to complain, criticize, and find fault with people and circumstances. You're just following the status quo since everybody seems to be doing it, but that is not a life with je ne sais quoi.

You are a queen. You have complete control over the inner critic that you listen to. You have a choice, in any given situation, over whether or not you will rule over your circumstances or let your circumstances rule over you. The power lies within your feminine, elegant self. You have it available to you right now. Despair no longer has to take the lead. Fear no longer has to hold you back. Doubt no longer has to be your default. Your decision to reign over your mindset is a matter of making the conscious choice to be intentional in how and what you think about throughout each day.

The chaotic world we live in is full of drama, negativity, anger, frustration, and depression. That is why powering your mindset requires perseverance and persistence. It's simple to spend the time in your day focused on positivity rather than negativity, but it may not always be easy. Some days you won't feel like doing it. Some days you won't think you need to do it. But the more frequently you supercharge your mindset with elegance, the stronger and more graceful it will become. When faced with a challenge or a difficult situation, your polished and positive mindset will give you the authority to stand firm in your beliefs that such situations will always have a favorable outcome.

BUILDING YOUR CLASSY CONFIDENCE

Confidence is your feeling of self-assuredness and certainty in yourself. And indeed, it's fueled by your mindset. Are you starting to realize that your mindset is running the show of your life? It's like the director on set — controlling the scene, characters, and script. When you are confident in yourself, you have positive beliefs about: who you are, how you define yourself, what you have to offer, and what you receive in life. A classy woman is a confident woman. To fully embrace confidence with class, your mindset has to be strong and steady – never wavering.

You wholeheartedly believe what you choose to believe – not sorta-kinda-almost believe – and you believe it all day, every day. You will need a strong mindset to preserve your confidence, as confidence is often tested during times of struggle or despair.

For example, if you aren't feeling well, then you make an appointment to visit your doctor. Sitting in the waiting room, wondering what in the world the doctor will say, you have a choice: you can either think positively or negatively. A thought from your positive conscience would be that the doctor will tell you that all you need to do is get extra rest and drink more water, but that you are healthy and won't require a follow-up appointment or prescription for medication. A thought from your negative conscience would be that you are sick with the flu or pneumonia, and you will need five shots and several prescriptions to get better.

What can negative thinking do to you? The same thing positive thinking can do: become your reality. If you are sitting in the waiting room before seeing the doctor, playing repeated thoughts that you are sick and will need medication, you can stress out your body to the point that it fulfills your thoughts, and you do end up making yourself ill. In contrast, you can think about how grateful you are for your health, which helps your body release tension, anxiety, and stress so that you can begin to relax and heal from within. A relaxed mind leads to a relaxed body. Your mindset is truly important because your thoughts are the foundation of your existence, right down to your well-being.

Before you say or do something, you likely thought about it first from your inner critic. Every action starts with a thought. Thoughts are like ripples in a pond, extending out from where a small stone was tossed in, creating additional sets of ripples on the surface of the water. Because your mind controls everything in your elegant life, you have to start the journey of confidence by first mastering your mindset. Your mindset can lead you to a happy, fulfilled, elegant, and refined life. Or your mindset can lead you to a depressed, dissatisfied, hectic, and tense life. The choice is ultimately yours. You decide which conscience you will listen to and the types of thoughts that you have. An elegant life with je ne sais quoi is always an option.

As you begin to master your mindset, you will find yourself brimming with confidence from head to toe. Confidence is truthfully the most stylish thing you can ever wear, and it always complements every outfit, just like a classic quilted Chanel handbag does! With confidence, you can achieve any goal and create a life that you'll love. Confidence fuels your ambition and motivation to live out your dreams, instead of staying stuck in fear, doubt, despair, or misery and wanting desperately to accomplish something but never pursuing it. If you want to sing the solo in the choir at church, you grab the microphone with poise. If you want to start a bakery, you sign up for cooking classes to perfect the skills for your delicious baked goods. If you want to overcome your fear of public speaking, you sign up for Toastmasters and gracefully stand in front of the room to deliver your weekly speeches.

This is the beginning of your life with je ne sais quoi. Confidence inspires you to pursue your passions with cultured, fearless, feminine flair. You'll graciously live with intention to delight in the activities of your life while operating with kindness and civility. Courtesy is the cousin of confidence. As you continue your journey of refining your life with je ne sais quoi, you'll learn that confidence and courtesy are always hand-in-hand, and your life will be much sweeter when you let them both guide your thoughts, actions, and interactions.

PONDER ON POSITIVITY

As we come to a close on exploring how to master your mindset, be encouraged that mastering your mindset is not a pass or fail endeavor, and it is certainly no small feat. Mastering your mindset is a lifelong journey. It will require daily fine-tuning to set your intention on optimism and keep your inner critic in check. Your morning routine of Gratitude Journaling will help to focus your mind on elegant thoughts. Some days you may have more positive thoughts than others, but you can always strive to search for the silver lining to surround your mind and life with pleasant energy and vibrations. Focus on the good in other people and situations, rather than leading with negativity, to create a life of je ne sais quoi.

A positive, healthy mindset and lifestyle come only from a continuous commitment to living with gratitude and seeking the good in life every single day. Mastering your mindset is not about making the decision one day to choose optimism; it's about deciding every day to choose optimism. As the dawn of each day unfolds a fresh morning, you are presented with an opportunity to strengthen your mindset elegantly, if you so choose And elegant thoughts create an elegant life.

Chic Mindset Secrets

- Acknowledge your two inner critics by their newly created names. Identify which inner critic you start listening to in any given situation, and let your positive conscience elegantly lead the way.

- Spend time every morning Gratitude Journaling by making a daily list in your journal of what you are grateful for.

- Live with optimism by considering the Elegant Mindset Question: "What is the good in this situation?" in a difficult moment to find the silver lining.

- Carry the sense of authority in your heart that you are capable of reigning over your mindset. You always have the power and the choice to choose elegance.

- Step out with confidence in all situations that frighten or intimidate you, knowing that you can achieve anything you set your mind to!

CHAPTER 2

GRACEFUL SELF-DISCOVERY

Knowing yourself is the beginning of all wisdom.

Aristotle

A life with je ne sais quoi shines with self-love. To know yourself is to love yourself. But how can you truly embrace elegance in your life without knowing the gorgeous woman in the mirror that gazes intently at you from your reflection? To confidently cross a room with your shoulders back and head held high, you must know all the elements that make you truly amazing, so your light can shine its brightest.

Every woman is perfectly imperfect. God did not create us without divinely choosing every single element of our personality, talents, hobbies, abilities, and dreams. It's all according to His plan, and He never makes mistakes. The decisions you make in life often define who you are, unless you take the time to define yourself first. Discovering who you are will give you confidence as you embrace the qualities you possess and lead with them instead of apologizing for flaws.

Self-discovery is the beautiful opportunity to take a long look in the mirror and find out who you truly are, beyond the superficialities of height, weight, hair color, and face shape. You are discovering yourself as a woman, with all your brilliance, strengths, goals, passions, and purpose.

This journey of self-discovery asks the mesmerizing question: Who are you? When is the last time you defined yourself without a familial or job title? We so often think of ourselves as wives, mothers, daughters, aunts, sisters, bankers, lawyers, realtors, teachers, and doctors. Family is indeed important, and you worked hard to accomplish all your professional accolades, but I challenge you to think of yourself as more than a family member or employee or entrepreneur. Look in the mirror and see yourself as a powerful woman who has feelings, thoughts, dreams, and passions.

If you're unsure of your dreams, ambitions, passions, or hobbies, now is the time to explore this uncharted territory. What makes you unique makes you beautiful. Without understanding who you are as a woman, you won't have the self-assurance necessary to leverage who you are to get what you want in life with elegance.

CONFIDENCE THROUGH CONSCIOUSNESS

In Chapter 1, Mastering Your Mindset, we explored how powerful your inner critics, thoughts, and beliefs are in your life. Confidence is like a rose with self-awareness as the stem. Confidence both develops and increases when we have a strong belief in our sense of self. When you know without a shadow of a doubt who you are and what you bring to the table, you find the power of being fully certain within yourself. I like to call this unshakable faith – the 1000% belief in yourself.

You can use this confidence to your advantage by willing your dreams and goals into reality with the Law of Attraction. After creating a thought, it enters the universe with energy from your vibration, or state of being. This can work to bring negative things your way if you have negative thoughts. For example, say you are waiting to hear back from the top-rated public relations agency after submitting your application for an Account Director position, and you keep thinking about how you probably aren't qualified for the role. The negative vibrations from your thoughts will adversely impact the outcome. But it can also work toward your favor. When you spend the majority of time focused on positivity, you will probably have more positive outcomes occur from your thoughts. For example, positive thoughts, like how you are the perfect candidate based on the fantastic results you got from your last client and the top-tier publicity skills you've spent the last fifteen years developing, send positive energy into the universe about the job opportunity.

You can align your dreams, passions, and goals with the thoughts you have about the outcome you want. Imagine yourself sitting in your new glass-walled office with a gorgeous view of the park outside. Your dreams and hopes should align with your thoughts so that you can fortify yourself with faith and tip the scales of every outcome in your favor.

Setting work aside for a moment, who is that gorgeous woman in the mirror? What are your dazzling dreams, passions, hobbies, and talents? Let's find out.

UNCOVERING YOUR TREASURED TALENTS

You have the honor of contributing to others while receiving delight and joy from spending time doing what you love. It is easy to take for granted the talents you have, assume that everyone else has them, or think that your skillset isn't valuable or worthy of recognition. That could not be further from the truth.

When you complete a task that you are good at doing and had fun completing, you feel the sense of accomplishment and satisfaction even after it's finished. That happy feeling of euphoria sprinkles a bit of charm and delight in your day. Discovering what you are good at doing is where we will begin the quest of self-discovery because celebrating your talents and skills is where the magic of living with je ne sais quoi will take form.

Every skill is worth celebrating, so find the joy in your talents and fully embrace them.

Actionable Advice

When you know your talents, you can refine and leverage them. Defining your skills helps you to start uncovering your elegant, accomplished self. In your journal, make a list titled "My Expertise" and write down a comprehensive catalog of each and every talent, skill, and strength you have. What are you naturally good at? What tasks can you do better than the average person? What things can you do that are so easy and effortless you could show someone how to do them in a snap?

Need some inspiration? Consider these examples below:

- Are you good at math?

- Can you change a tire in a flash?

- Do you have an eye for interior design and coordinating rooms with stylish flair?

- Are you awesome at explaining a difficult concept to someone, making it easy and simple?

- Can you write HTML or JavaScript?

- Do you sing well, always carrying a lovely tune?

- Are you gifted with a paintbrush, oil paints, and canvas?

Write every skill and strength you have, no matter how big or small or even silly you think it is. You can complete this journal exercise in one session or pause as needed and return to continue developing your master list of talents and skills. Continue writing all your talents and skills until you've included all the things you can think of that you do well and effortlessly.

Once you complete your list of expertise, have a look at it for review. When is the last time you did some of the things you were good at? Has it been a few days, weeks, or even years since you used some of your expertise?

The areas in which you are highly skilled are a gift from God and, as we learned earlier, have been placed within you by divine order. Once you identify them, it's important to remember all the skills and talents that you have, because that is a huge part of defining your chic, gifted self! You can now acknowledge your talent and brilliance.

Review your list of expertise often for a polished pick-me-up to remind yourself of how multi-talented you truly are. Be inspired to find opportunities to apply your vast expertise when situations in your life arise.

* * * * *

PURSUING YOUR PASSIONS

Passion is defined as, "an intense desire or enthusiasm for something," according to the New Oxford American Dictionary. It's a feeling of radiance and vibrancy from within, very similar to happiness (with an extra dash of sparkle!). A life with je ne sais quoi is full of positivity, excitement, and certainly passion.

Passion is the energetic sense of bringing positive energy to what you're doing. With passion, you have positive energy in every area of your life. You have excitement and zest in every single day. Without passion, your life will be missing the sparkle it was meant to have for you to shine fully.

Passion is important because without it you can spend your entire life doing things you don't genuinely enjoy. Without passion, you probably feel like you're not living your best life. And there is no point in living each day unfulfilled, feeling like you are hanging by a thread. An empty life can lead to miserable months, years, and even decades of *doing* but not *living*! One sign you are living an unfulfilled life is if you always seem to be rushing around and are constantly 'busy,' but you truly wish you were spending your time on something else. Your heart and intuition will tell you if you are living enriched and satisfied, or unfulfilled and empty.

A life with passion is like a pair of Jimmy Choo slingbacks; complete, each heel needing the other to thrive. Your talent is like the left shoe while your passion is the right shoe. Two shoes are great separately, but they're much better together. Just like two single shoes, talent and passion are better together (they create your life purpose, after all!).

It is so easy to get caught up in the activities of daily life—managing your career, social calendar, and family—that you can easily forget the simple things. A winning moment you can give yourself any time you have a spare minute or two available is to spend time enjoying your passion.

Find what you love and do what you love.

Actionable Advice

Now that you've uncovered your expertise, skills, and strengths you have as natural talents, it is time to review your list and determine what you truly enjoy. When God places a skill within you, and you enjoy using that skill, you have a rare gift that is meant to be shared, not kept to yourself in secret. The things you enjoy are what you can and should be doing to live the best version of your life fully.

I encourage you to pull out your expertise list and find a highlighter pen. As you review each talent and skill that you've written down, ask yourself what you are good at doing that you also **love** to do. What can you do exceptionally well that makes you feel invigorated as if you come alive when doing it?

Perhaps you can solve mathematical equations, but you get bored staring at a spreadsheet full of numbers.

Or maybe you can change tires better than anyone else you know, but it doesn't excite you to pull the wheel off a Mercedes-Benz coupe.

But maybe, when coordinating a kitchen design with contemporary tiles and modern appliances, the spark within you is ignited.

Or perhaps when teaching a challenging concept to someone, you enjoy it so much that you simply lose track of time.

As you review your expertise list, be sure to highlight **only** the talents on your list that you absolutely adore!

The highlighted items on your expertise list are what you are passionate about, a sweet marriage of both skills and interest.

This chapter is called Graceful Self-Discovery because it involves reflecting on tough yet honest questions to uncover the truth of who you are, thereby giving yourself the freedom to find the answers without being critical or judgmental. The investigation into your passions should be both fun and rewarding.

Now, take a look at the highlighted items on your list. Ask yourself, "How often do I do these things?" If you love to write code (and you're amazing at it), why don't you make time in your schedule to do so? What is stopping you or holding you back from doing the things you are both good at doing and also enjoy?

It's time for a challenge! Select one passion from your expertise list that you can make time to enjoy at least once a week. Even if you give yourself just a few minutes or even an hour, I challenge you to make time to do something you love. You may be surprised that your passion can inspire you in ways you would never have dreamed of. Life has an interesting way of teaching us lessons, and often the ones we value the most happen when we least expect them.

* * * * *

FINDING YOUR PURPOSE

God created every one of us on this planet with a purpose. We are here for a divine reason, even if we have yet to discover it. Some theorists believe we have only one purpose (like having only one true soulmate) while others believe we can have multiple purposes.

Regardless of which theory you choose to believe, realize that you do have at least one reason for being created and existing.

Do you know your life's purpose?

The best way to discover your life purpose, if you don't already know it, is to explore your passions and interests. Somewhere in the mix is your purpose because you are blessed with passions and interests for a reason; you just have to combine them to unlock their purposeful power.

You can explore your passions by stepping outside your normal comfort zone and serving new people with your passions. Once you follow your passions and see where they lead you, you will be able to be open to what you find. Regardless of what you do or who you help, you can learn what you like and don't like about each particular passion or interest, just from spending time in the activity.

I suggest you embark on one new adventure every month to pursue using a passion or interest, especially the activities that pique your curiosity that you have not yet explored. If you love French cuisine and have an interest in cooking, that may mean you sign up for a cooking class at a local bistro. If you love animals and have a passion for puppies, that may mean you volunteer at the local Humane Society.

Actionable Advice

Keep an entry in your journal each month on the progress of pursuing your passions and interests, logging how you feel and what you think about each experience.

After trying new things, you might be pleasantly surprised by what the experience was really like (and how skillful you happen to be!).

* * * * *

Discovering your purpose doesn't happen overnight, but once you come across what you love to do and are brilliantly amazing at, you'll feel the difference – the spark will ignite! You will know when you find your purpose because you'll receive mental, physical, and emotional confirmation. You will feel the alignment of power and purpose. You'll light up when you talk about your purpose. You'll smile when you think about fulfilling your purpose. You'll constantly develop ideas for improvements and create new approaches to explore. Your heart will let you know once you've found your life purpose, and you'll feel within your spirit the feeling that *this is it*!

Actionable Advice

Once you've identified your passion or passions, write them in your journal on a separate page.

For your inspiration, you can fill in the blanks using the phrases mentioned below:

I am an expert at _____, _____, _____, and _____.

(Fill in the blanks with your top four talents from your list of expertise, based on what you are the best at from your comprehensive list of skills.)

My passions include _____, _____, and _____.

(Fill in the blanks with your top three passions. These are things you are interested in and also enjoy doing.)

My life purpose is _____.

(Fill in the blank with your life purpose. This is similar to a life mission statement. What do you do well and enjoy doing, who does it help, and how does it impact others? Answering those three questions, in whatever order you see fit, will inspire you to write down your life purpose.)

* * * * *

Whether you pursue your life purpose as a career or for enjoyment instead of income, your life will feel more enriched and worthwhile once you identify and live within your purpose. Life is meant to be enjoyed, and fulfilling your purpose is one of many ways to enjoy all the beauty life has to offer.

CREATING YOUR CHIC SELF

So far on this wonderful journey of self-discovery, you've uncovered your unique talents, passions, and purpose. Now let's put it all together.

You can be defined by many different things: your experiences, education, family, career, talents, passions and purpose. But how do *you* define yourself? Consider this — if you had to think of just one word to describe yourself, what would it be? Without thinking about how *others* would label you: how would *you* label yourself? How you define yourself is the most essential definition of all.

When you look in the mirror, who do you see? The question isn't *what* you see on the exterior, not your enchanting blush or bombshell curls or chic Hermès scarf, but the lady within. *Who* do you see?

The labels you place upon yourself as a woman can either help or hurt your confidence. This is when confidence emerges from behind the red velvet curtains and takes center stage in your life. Your beliefs about yourself affect every element of your life – what you say, what you do, how you say things, how you interact with others. Essentially, the way you show up in life puts your confidence on full display. The most compelling thing about defining yourself is that, once you do, you can position yourself confidently so that others will know the true you.

Defining yourself is an important exercise in becoming attuned to who you truly are. You know your talents, passions, and purpose, and you know what you are capable of doing, but what do you want to be known for?

Actionable Advice

Spend time in reflection with your journal and write down all the words you can think of that would be flattering if someone paid you a compliment using them.

What are all the words with which you want other people to associate with you?

Think of it this way: you have just walked by a group of people at a dinner party, someone says your name, and another person says, "Oh I know her, she's _____." What word would you want them to use? What word could someone use to describe you that would make you feel proud, honored, and delighted to be thought of in that way?

In this brainstorm, include every word on your list that would be precious praise for someone to describe you with.

After creating a list of at least twenty descriptor words on a master list, choose one. Just one word. Reflect on the one word that stands out from the list, the one you are moved by, the one your heart is drawn to. The one word that embodies your full essence.

Once you have the one word that describes *you* – not your glamorous wardrobe, not your dedicated work ethic, not your enchanting personality – you as a woman, circle it in your journal.

Write in your journal: I, [your name goes here] am _____.

Defining yourself is a major breakthrough in self-discovery, and as such, it should be a process that is thoughtfully regarded, not rushed. If you have to spend more than one session in your journal until you come up with the one word that both inspires and motivates you, spend all the time you need to find the word that embodies you. There is no deadline. Instead, be thoughtful and spend as long as is necessary until you feel comfortable with the one special word that defines you.

* * * * *

Your one word that defines you? That should be the one word that drives you.

Your word isn't an accessory, like the perfect strand of pearls, but rather, it's a clarification. Everything you think, say, do, and wear should be in alignment with your defining word. When you define who you are and want others to see you the way that you see yourself, what you say and do must be congruent with your word.

Every day going forward, whatever word you chose, I encourage you to be intentional in your life. Before you think, say, or do something, verify that your action *supports* instead of *devalues* how you define yourself.

For example, if you define yourself as a loyal woman, then you wouldn't spend time at your family reunion making public a secret your sister told you in confidence. It wouldn't make sense to define yourself as loyal and then directly discredit your loyalty to your sister by regularly engaging in the exact opposite behavior, gossiping.

LIVING WITH GRACEFUL INTENTION

Notice that in the previous exercise, you were proactive in defining yourself. You took the initiative and leveraged your complete power and control to define how you want others to regard you. You did not allow others to define you with their opinions, so you could follow their lead. You defined yourself with the one word that impresses, awes, and inspires you.

The influence that word has should be within every area of your life, from what you say to what you do, to what you think. Especially what you think. When you imagine the elegant woman you want to be, whatever doesn't match up in your life with that image is what you should look to change, thereby elevating yourself to be elegant in every area of your life. If you want to be a person who is kind to others but, in a stressful situation with a cashier at Saks Fifth Avenue, you're snapping and yelling, then you're not being kind. In other words, your actions aren't matching up with your intentions.

Here's a chic life secret: to live honorably, the lady you hope to be and the lady you actually are should be the same person.

Ultimate confidence will come from being the lady that you want to be—a dynamic woman that acknowledges and appreciates her talents, passions, and purpose. To experience life with full confidence and authority, strive to be the best woman you can be in all circumstances and situations. That way, every evening when you look in the mirror, you will smile proudly, thinking of the one word that defines you and every moment of your day that made it true. And because none of us are ever perfect, the most elegant thing you can do is strive to live out the characteristics associated with your one word by living gracefully, with intention.

REFINEMENT WITH AFFIRMATIONS

After you have decided on the word that defines who you want to be, it's helpful to reinforce and reaffirm yourself to fuel your feminine power. Writing affirmations, which are positive phrases of encouragement, and placing them in a location that you will regularly see them, gives you a sparkle of positive energy and boosts your confidence. Affirmations are an amazing way to remind yourself of the beautiful, strong, smart, confident woman that you are. It's also an inspired way to bless yourself with an extra dose of sunshine when faced with a difficult challenge or a day when you simply aren't feeling your best. We all have 'gray days,' and affirmations are a beautifully delicate reminder that can help you turn up your light to let it shine.

Actionable Advice

Find five 3' x 5' index cards and write down an affirmation phrase on each one. On the first index card, write your life purpose or purposes. On the second index card, write the word that defines you. For the remaining three index cards, write a power statement on each card to give you a spark of joy and motivation.

A few affirmation examples include:

- "I am confident and capable of gracefully handling every challenge I encounter."

- "I am who I decide and define."

- "I am divine perfection. I know who I am."

You can place these five index cards on your bedroom dresser, tape them on your bathroom mirror, or keep them in your handbag for easy reference.

The power that affirmations hold is in their ability to inspire you from repeated viewing. Every morning after completing your Gratitude Journaling, find these affirmations and read them aloud. Stand proudly, shoulders back, head held high, and read them with conviction.

This is how you can powerfully start each day and prepare yourself to operate within the realm of your feminine greatness.

* * * * *

Out of all the time you spend in a day on various activities, you should reserve at least a few minutes for yourself. After getting to know who you are through self-exploration, be sure to reinforce positivity in your talented, elegant self with daily affirmations for a quick reminder of your purpose, value, and worth.

Chic Self Secrets

- Apply the Law of Attraction to your dreams, hopes, and goals. Spend time focusing on positive elements that bring you closer to achieving and accomplishing what you want in life.

- Once your life purpose is identified, live intentionally by making it a priority to fulfill it. There are always people in need of the unique talents and skills you have to offer.

- Make time each month to explore a new passion or interest you are curious to try out. In the process, you may uncover a hidden talent you didn't realize you had.

- Take the initiative to define who you want to be, and then live according to those principles to be elegantly in alignment.

- Read your affirmations daily each morning after Gratitude Journaling. This is your way to have power and poise in your morning routine.

CHAPTER 3

CHOOSING HAPPINESS

No one can make you feel inferior without your consent.

Eleanor Roosevelt

How do you define happiness? We often measure our happiness based on our circumstances: how much money we have, who we are dating or married to, and what part of town we live in. When life is going well, we are so-called 'happy.'

But happiness isn't about attaining wealth, being with the perfect gentleman, or having a house in a gated, popular neighborhood. Happiness is far deeper than the tangible things in our lives. Happiness is the sense of positive well-being and satisfaction that you wholeheartedly feel in both your head and your heart. I like to think of happiness as the positive feeling of contentment. When you are content, you aren't necessarily ecstatic or overjoyed—you are at peace. You have a feeling of pleasant tranquility.

Some people define happiness as a mood that comes and goes, but on the contrary, happiness is a combination of experiencing joy and realizing that life is both worthwhile and meaningful. Happiness is having a peaceful, positive state of mind. Although you may not feel joyful and ecstatic every moment throughout each day, you can be happy with a generally pleasant presence every day. Happy women don't necessarily spend all day smiling, laughing, or with high energy; but they do carry themselves with a pleasant composure, cherishing the winning moments they have, and finding satisfaction in each day.

Happiness is important because the quality of our lives is entirely determined by what we continuously think and feel. As we explored in Chapter 1, Mastering Your Mindset, your mindset has massive power and affects every area of your life because your thoughts become actions, and your actions motivate your interactions. Before we have thoughts, we have feelings. The way you *feel* influences everything in your life, so if your thoughts are the director of the show of your life, then your feelings are like the producer that manages all the high-level decisions like hiring the director and crew on set. How you feel (good or bad) will influence your thoughts (good or bad), which influences your actions (good or bad), and your actions lead to interactions with other people (good or bad). If feelings are the core, the very foundation of everything in our lives, then how we judge and measure the quality of our lives is dependent on feelings, too. And happiness is a feeling.

Women are commonly stereotyped as 'emotional beings' – which is true. All humans are emotional beings. Men are also emotional beings, but we as women are often more in tune with how we feel compared to men. By being aware of how your emotions affect your state of mind and perspective, you can prevent yourself from being controlled by those same emotions. Instead, you can use those captivating emotions as intuitive cues that help you react with more positivity and kindness to find joy in difficult situations.

How you *feel* about a person or situation is important because it dictates what you will *do* about it. Every action, positive or negative, has a consequence – an outcome or result that occurs. Choosing happiness means you choose a positive state of mind, and when you are happy you can easily handle adversity with grace and poise.

THE POWER OF CHOICE

No person in the world can force you to feel a certain way. You choose your feelings. As frustrating as it may be when a person deceives or disrespects you, you get to walk away from the situation with full control over how you will feel. You can choose anger and resentment or grace and compassion.

I am not suggesting you become a doormat and let people say and do things that wreak havoc on your life. I am suggesting, however, that you choose positive actions over negative ones. I encourage you to look for the good in every situation and train yourself to choose peace instead of anxiety consistently.

A few examples may help to clarify how you can choose happiness in any situation, regardless of how unfortunate the circumstance may be. Often in life, difficulty is an opportunity that challenges you to rely on your strength and develop resilience. Upon spraining your ankle, you can take heart that you are alive and be thankful that each day of healing brings you one step closer to full recovery. Upon being laid off from a job, you can find solace in the fact that you now have the opportunity to explore new employment options, and you can expand your horizons by switching to a new job role or a new company. After a bad breakup, separation or divorce, you can embrace this new chapter in your life as a fresh start and see it as a new beginning.

Keep in mind that a life with je ne sais quoi is a life dancing to the tune of optimism. Life experiences are certain to carry both positive and negative circumstances, but your feelings about them will influence how you react. The type of life you want to live is entirely within your control. You can't control every situation, but you can control your emotions and actions in every situation. You have the pleasure of choosing the quality of life you will have. Be intentional in the choices that you select each day.

Choosing happiness elevates your elegance.

You can choose to practice regulating your emotions because you know that the happiness of a gracious, peaceful life will elevate your elegance.

A life with je ne sais quoi is not an average, mundane life full of never-ending gray days and sadness.

You are not a victim; you are a victor (if you choose to be!). When you realize that being thoughtful and living with intention means choosing happiness, you're exerting effort that will elevate how you think, feel, speak, and live. If you want to create an elegant life for yourself, it's going to require you to make a bit more effort than the average Jane, and since you're reading this book, I know you're up for the challenge.

Think of it this way; to practice law after graduating from law school, you first have to pass the bar exam. If you want to be a lawyer, you know that committing significant hours toward studying for the bar exam is just part of the process. In a sense, it's what you signed up for the day you enrolled in your first law school class. Similarly, if you want to live with elegance, you'll have to make an effort daily to create the life you want – choosing happiness is part of the process.

Over time, choosing to be happy becomes a simple feat. But when initially forming any new habit, it takes more energy and focus to establish the routine than to maintain it once it's a habit.

A Chic Reminder

> Gratitude inspires happiness. As you establish the new habit of choosing happiness in your life, I recommend committing to Gratitude Journaling, your morning routine of journaling for reflection and gratitude, as mentioned in Chapter 1, Mastering Your Mindset. By making time every day to focus on the positive elements in your life, it will help you to feel better, regardless of what circumstance you may be dealing with on any given day.

Happiness is a journey, not a destination. With the dawn of each new day, you have the illustrious opportunity to choose happiness. Focusing on the positive elements in your daily life presents you with a gift: the opportunity to choose happiness. As you get into the groove of your new, happy, elegant life, you will find that it becomes easier to choose happiness as a habit you take part in daily, like brushing your hair every evening before bed.

One common misconception is that once you are happy, you continue to stay happy. On the contrary, you must continue choosing happiness to maintain it. That's because happiness is a mental state that you must consciously bring to every situation and life encounter you face. Just like maintaining good dental hygiene keeps your dazzling smile bright, you deliberately brush and floss your teeth every day. To maintain your happiness and keep your life polished and poised, you'll have to carefully select your thoughts and set your intention on choosing happiness.

CULTIVATING HAPPINESS

Happiness also contributes to your ability to achieve personal ambitions. Happiness supports confidence.

When you are happy, you are more likely to make the considerable effort required toward accomplishing your goals. We often measure the quality of our lives based on the successes that we achieve; therefore, happiness reinforces our ability to live a high quality of life, as well.

Happiness can be influenced in many ways. Believe it or not, happiness is the positive state of mind that serves as our default. We are naturally wired to be happy. But from the moment we open our eyes to greet a new day, life can and does throw a massive amount of challenges our way that can easily trigger depression, fear, anger, and anxiety.

One way to cultivate happiness is to let go of negativity. Negative thoughts (like self-doubt, worry, and dissatisfaction) have no place in your mind, spirit, or body. When you release negativity and don't allow it to occupy space in your head or heart, the only thing that remains is contentment and peace of mind – happiness. Turning off the voice from your negative conscience will help you to create a happy and graceful life.

Releasing negativity is often easier said than done. But once you start releasing negativity, it becomes effortless over time and often transforms into an innate activity without you having to focus energy on it consciously. Metaphorically speaking, you have to empty your cup to make room for something else to fill it. Removing negativity for the long-term is best achieved by replacing negative thoughts with positive thoughts.

Actionable Advice

A focus on positivity is one of the most common ways to cultivate happiness.

Happiness is about peace, joy, and contentment. It's not about being jovial or goofy, but it's about having a pleasant feeling about circumstances and experiences. You can't change some things that occur, but you can change your mindset and attitude by choosing to be happy and carrying joy in your heart every day. You can choose to be content in all situations.

JE NE SAIS QUOI

In the moments when you feel lethargic and uninspired throughout the day or evening, find your journal and spend a few minutes writing all the things that bring you happiness, joy, and peace. I like to call this Joy Journaling. Nothing is too big or small to recognize. Waking up to see another day is something to be joyful about, and if it's a rainy day, well, rain is known as liquid sunshine and is the very source that flowers, trees, and plants need to quench their thirst. Did I mention that a rainy day is an excuse to wear your stylish Ted Baker parka? See how this works? It's finding the silver lining in anything that occurs in life and thus, choosing happiness.

If, during tough times, negative thoughts creep into your mind as you journal about your joy, ask yourself the Elegant Mindset Question: "What is the good in this situation?" and write all your thoughts, rephrased as positive instead of negative.

Spend just a few moments thinking happy thoughts during an unfortunate time on a given day, to fill your cup with positivity. This is a worthwhile exercise that can help you to focus on all the good things in life, even on the most difficult of days.

* * * * *

A gracious life is
a gratified life.

A delightful life is a life with happiness. You may not feel happy every moment in a day, but you *can* be happy every day. One thing is certain, and that is that life is a mixed bag of experiences. But the way you handle situations and respond to challenges influences your feelings, thoughts, and actions, and thus your quality of life. Happiness is a state of mind, and although life is a roller coaster, you can maintain a pleasant and even temper throughout situations both good and bad, bringing happiness with you along for the ride! Your sense of contentment and peace of mind will even help you to navigate through adversity when negative situations occur. Happiness can help you always to take the high road when difficulties arise. Controlling your emotions takes practice, but practice makes perfect.

Living with grace will give you satisfaction. Grace is an empowering level of peace from a transcendent awareness in a situation. You display grace when you may not be able to control a situation but choose to make the most of it; when you have courteous goodwill toward others during a challenging time; and when you rise above your frustration and disappointment in interactions with others.

Imagine you're at home, cuddled up on your tufted couch with a glass of champagne and a plate of crackers and cheese, watching your favorite television show. It's the last sixty seconds of the episode, and it ends with a stunning cliffhanger! As you gasp in shock that the main character is involved in a thrilling plot twist, you fail to pay attention to your two-year-old daughter. She playfully tosses her toy into the air…and breaks your grandmother's beloved vase, an expensive and treasured family heirloom. In this situation, you might be sorely tempted to lose it, yelling to reprimand your toddler. But being gracious demands that you rise above the calamity. Grace requires you to recognize that your daughter is just a child playing with her toys, and she didn't intend to cause any harm or damage. Although you're upset, explosive anger is not appropriate.

When you have the self-awareness necessary to evaluate any given circumstance, you can choose a graceful response and maintain a level of happiness, even when you lose something precious that you held near and dear to your heart. Giving into anger or fear in a difficult moment will deprive you of joy and deplete your sense of elegance. In the above example, choosing to react to your child with kindness will make you happy and take heart in the fact that you are living out your values as a compassionate mother.

HOW HAPPINESS AFFECTS CONFIDENCE

Happiness affects your self-esteem. When you are happy, you also tend to feel good about yourself. Being optimistic in your life leads to feeling satisfied with yourself. Confidence helps you to maintain your happiness because when you recognize your strength from within, you can face any challenge or difficult situation with gravitas and grace. Instead of uncertainty in yourself, you hold the firm belief that you are capable of achieving and accomplishing anything you strive to pursue.

Confidence also supports conquering your fears and practicing resilience. You can overcome confidently every single challenge that you may encounter with dignity instead of despair.

THE BENEFITS OF HAPPINESS

Happiness leads to positive feelings, overall well-being, and a higher quality of life. When you give positivity the priority in your life, choosing happiness becomes easier. After making the conscious effort over time to consistently choose happiness, you will be able to choose happiness unconsciously. This reflexive choice is what I like to call your Happiness Instinct, your ability to choose happiness almost automatically without exerting considerable effort.

Happiness is one of the many ingredients to creating a life with je ne sais quoi. When you are happy, you feel better physically and emotionally, you look better, and all of your abilities are heightened. Happy people are more compassionate and kinder toward others, have more enriched relationships, and achieve more success in their career endeavors.

Another added benefit of happiness is that it is contagious. As a happy woman, when you are kind and happy during interactions with others, you give them the gift of happiness. They will be happier, too. You've probably heard the phrase before that misery loves company; well, happiness also pines for a companion!

Happiness isn't just for you — it's for everyone around you.

A life with happiness allows you to create the elegant life that you want. Happiness is an opportunity for you to live with fulfillment and satisfaction every day. Your dreams are always within reach when you choose happiness. The choice lies in front of you, in every encounter, situation, and circumstance. Choose wisely.

Chic Happiness Secrets

- Happiness is having a peaceful, positive state of mind.

- You may not be happy all day, every day, but you can choose to be happy every day.

- Happiness is not a one-and-done choice you make. You must consistently choose happiness to elevate your life with elegance.

- Being happy fortifies your confidence and boosts your ability to be a graceful woman conquering your dreams, hopes, wishes, and fears.

- When you feel uninspired from a day that you don't feel your best, enjoy a session of Joy Journaling to reflect and write in your journal about all the things that bring you joy.

PART 2
CARE

CHAPTER 4

PERSONAL STYLE

*Dress shabbily
and they remember the dress.
Dress impeccably
and they remember the woman.*

Coco Chanel

Your style is the first thing that someone notices about you. Consider this: it's early Saturday morning, and you're headed to the florist to get your weekly bouquet of fresh loveliness to adorn your kitchen table. You roll out of bed, get dressed, and walk down the street to the flower shop. As you enter the store and walk to the left side where the peonies are, you hear someone call your name. As you turn your head to the right…you are greeted by your boss, Cynthia, and her husband, Tom. This was *not* what you were expecting at 8 AM on a Saturday, and you embarrassingly cling to your sweatshirt, pulling it down to cover the alfredo sauce stain on the left thigh of your hole-riddled, see-through yoga pants.

Has a situation like that ever occurred in your life? Have you ever had *outfit remorse*?

A life with je ne sais quoi is about creating and wearing your personal style to visually display your *best* self, all in a respectable and tasteful manner. It's no secret that when you wear an outfit that you are proud of, you are both confident and comfortable. You walk proudly into a room and own it, with a delightful smile, head held high, and shoulders pushed back. You own every moment of your day with feminine power when you're sporting your personal style.

I know you've heard the adage, "You are what you eat." but realize this — you are also what you *wear*. Clothing and accessories that you wear are non-verbal communication, visual signals to display who you are to those around you. People will perceive you based on how you present yourself. A rushed morning may cause you to get dressed frantically before heading out the door, but attire with food stains, lint, or a foul odor is not a respectable way to present yourself. People that encounter you in that outfit will assume you are sloppy, unorganized, and lazy.

Your sense of personal style, the look of the clothing and accessories you wear, is completely your prerogative. If you prefer pastel colors and looser fabrics over neutral colors and structured materials, you can still build an authentic wardrobe that fits your personal style <u>and</u> personal taste. The key thing to remember about your wardrobe is that it is a form of communication, so you want to give intention to what you wear so you can communicate your desired message. Every piece in your wardrobe should be something you love that represents your personality and showcases your elegance.

Style allows you to influence the power of perception.

Another aphorism you've likely heard before is that, "perception is reality." Perception plays a large role in how people decide to interact with one another. The way people perceive you is who they will assume you are.

The decisions for a new job opportunity, a romantic relationship, and even friendships are influenced by the thoughts a person has about you. The perception people have of you motivates their decisions in deciding to hire, promote, date, marry, or befriend you. Which type of woman do you think people want to hire, marry, or become friends with: a sophisticated woman or a sloppy woman? Is a sophisticated woman or a sloppy woman more likely to excel in a new job role? Is a sophisticated woman or a sloppy woman more likely to make a positive impression with clients and customers? Is a sophisticated woman or a sloppy woman more likely to make a good life partner? Is a sophisticated woman or a sloppy woman more likely to be a kind and encouraging friend? These questions are what others are considering about you before they extend a new opportunity to you, whether it's impacting your professional or personal life.

The two most important elements about your elegant personal style are tastefulness and authenticity.

TASTEFULNESS

Your wardrobe should always be tasteful. Tastefulness is all about being appropriate to wear something suitable for the variety of activities in your life: work, exercise, errands, socializing, fine dining, and formal celebrations. Dress codes are established for various events and locations to create a level of consideration for how people should dress in order to be tasteful. Wearing appropriate attire for every occasion presents yourself with dignity and will also earn you the respect of others.

Regardless of what personal style best fits your personality, you can properly display yourself with elegance by wearing clothing that is appropriate for every occasion and presents you in a respectful manner. Instead of dressing with your midriff, bosom, or derrière exposed, be intentional with your appearance to present yourself respectfully. When you show that you respect your body and keep the focus on you instead of your assets, you display a good sense of taste. Wearing a blouse that's too low cut simply because it was sold to you that way or wearing booty shorts or a bodycon dress just because they're in style shows a lack of taste. Don't be a victim of fad fashion and other people's bad choices.

Can you imagine walking into an investment bankers' networking mixer wearing flip-flops, cut-off shorts, a low-bearing tank top, and a hair scrunchie? Perhaps you can imagine it. Perhaps you have done it. Imagining the look of shock, and maybe horror on the face of just one executive from a prestigious bank upon seeing you walk in should be enough to deter you from this. The appropriate attire for work and work-related events is very different from the appropriate attire you would wear to the gym for a Pilates class (unless you happen to work at a gym as a personal trainer!).

AUTHENTICITY

In addition to your wardrobe always being tasteful, your wardrobe should always be authentic. Personal style is personal. The clothing and accessories you wear should accurately reflect both your personality and your demeanor, the woman you are.

Creating your personal style starts with creating your Elegant Style Personality. To do this, consider an answer to the question: "What personality do I want my appearance to have?" Instead of thinking about the personality traits you have, think about the personality you want your style to convey. What is the one word you want your style to say about you to others?

Your personality may be goofy because you love to make people laugh, but your appearance should never make you look like a joke. Instead, you can find a more subdued yet whimsical way to communicate your light-hearted demeanor with your outfit, like a colorful scarf or brightly colored satchel. Your personality may be serious because you like to be direct and get straight to the point with others, but your appearance should not be so severe that it's off-putting. Instead of always dressing in solid black and navy from head-to-toe, softening the look with a dainty accent piece, such as a cream silk blouse or pair of tan pointy-toe pumps can be just the right addition to your outfit, allowing you to express your personality with a touch of approachable style.

There are a variety of personal style types that fit different personalities, each showcasing various personality traits and characteristics. The colors, fabrics, type of clothing, and accessories you wear every day should be authentic to your personality and accurately show who you are to others. Your wardrobe should be an accurate reflection of yourself for the sole purpose of accentuating you. You have the pleasure of deciding what you wear, so why not make getting dressed one of your most enjoyable parts of the day? By wearing clothing that you love that authentically represents who you are; you will feel more confident and radiate your fully beautiful self to the world!

Your wardrobe can be tasteful and authentic, but it won't just happen on its own. You will have to be intentional, spending time to create a personal style that best fits your lifestyle and your personality. The good news is, it is easier than you think. You won't have to spend countless hours aimlessly guessing how to create the perfect wardrobe for yourself. With the guidance in this book, you can delightfully be intentional when choosing pieces for your wardrobe to ensure you have a curated collection of clothing and accessories for every event and occasion in your life.

Everything you wear should have a purpose.

Developing your personal style is an ever-evolving journey. Today, you may decide you want your

Elegant Style Personality to be Bold and Edgy, but in five years, you may decide you want your Elegant Style Personality to be Classic and Timeless. We are all only human, which means change is inevitable. Your style should change with you. As you mature and evolve throughout your life, your style should always reflect who you currently are. The woman you are today should be reflected through the current wardrobe that you have hanging beautifully in your closet right now.

Actionable Advice

Atop a fresh page in your journal, write the title, "My Personality." Make a list including all the personality traits and characteristics that you use to define yourself. Then think about the answer to this question: "How would my best friend describe me?" While your self-defining adjectives are from your internal perspective, your best friend is the one person who knows you better than almost anyone and has an external perspective.

Your list of personality traits can be as long or as short as you'd like.

After your comprehensive list of personality traits is complete, circle the one characteristic from your list that you cherish the most and which defines your personality. It is the <u>one</u> way to describe yourself that feels the most genuine and authentic.

Now it's time to define your Elegant Style Personality.

Turn to a fresh page in your journal and write the title "My Elegant Style Personality" at the top. List all the descriptive words that you want your wardrobe to convey about you. You can have fun with this! How would you want someone to describe your appearance? Your Elegant Style Personality is how you want to be viewed by others and is aligned with who you are as a woman. When your brainstorm is complete, circle the <u>one</u> characteristic from your list that you want to describe your appearance.

Your personality characteristic and your Elegant Style Personality should not be the same word. For example, if your personality characteristic is "Generous," your Elegant Style Personality should not also be "Generous." But, if your personality characteristic is "Generous," and you want to be viewed by others as kind, caring, and feminine, then perhaps your Elegant Style Personality is "Classic" or "Dainty."

Once you choose the one word for your personality and your Elegant Style Personality, write the following in your journal, filling in the blanks with the words you have selected for each category.

My personality is _____.

My Elegant Style Personality is _____.

* * * * *

WHAT'S YOUR STYLE PERSONALITY?

Below is a broad list of style personalities to inspire you as you're defining your Elegant Style Personality.

Relaxed & Casual

This Elegant Style Personality is ideal for the lady most comfortable in jeans and a t-shirt. Your ideal outfit includes two pieces—a top and a bottom. You like a variety of different prints and solid colors, including pastels and neutrals, but you're not a fan of neon colors. Your makeup is neutral if you wear any at all.

Bold & Edgy

This Elegant Style Personality is ideal for the lady happiest in dark, bold, or neon colors. You enjoy wearing soft concert t-shirts and structured fabrics, like leather and menswear-inspired pieces. You are more likely to wear a jumpsuit instead of a dress to a formal event. Pushing limits and fashion rules gets your blood pumping, and your ideal closet is full of trendy, couture, avant-garde, and eclectic pieces. Your makeup always includes dark eyeliner, for both day and night.

Simple & Minimalist

This Elegant Style Personality is ideal for the lady who loves an easy wardrobe, so getting dressed in the morning is short and sweet! You crave order in your closet and like wearing pants, skirts, and cardigans that can be mixed and matched. You always gravitate toward solid, neutral colors – white, black, navy and gray – with very few patterns, if any. Your makeup is neutral with a pop of color for your lipstick.

Romantic & Feminine

This Elegant Style Personality is ideal for the lady who prefers skirts and dresses over pants and can't live without romantic peasant blouses and blouson dresses. Your ideal closet is full of pastel colors, flowy fabrics, ruffles, A-line dresses, and anything that feels delicate, including silk, chiffon, and lace. Your makeup is dewy and fresh with a glowing finish, and you always include a shade of pink for lipstick.

Classic & Timeless

This Elegant Style Personality is ideal for the lady who prefers structured fabrics and dressy outfits with at least three pieces. Your closet is stocked with pearls, blazers, silk blouses, sheath dresses, A-line dresses, neck scarves, pumps, dress pants, and dark-wash denim jeans. Your ideal color palette consists of neutrals worn with one print at a time (if any print is worn at all). The one print you can't live without in your closet is stripes. Your makeup consists of natural colors for eyes and cheeks, with a corresponding lipstick color for each season.

Boho & Whimsical

This Elegant Style Personality is ideal for the lady who can't go a week without wearing a maxi skirt or dress. Your idea of a fun outfit is anything with fringe, tassel earrings, long pendant necklaces, and handmade rings and bracelets set with turquoise and other earth stones, of course! Your closet is filled with maxi skirts, maxi dresses, duster jackets, halter dresses, and flared pants, all in earth tone colors like browns, greens, whites, creams, and blues. Your favorite prints are floral, paisley, tribal plaid, and geometric. Your makeup is dewy and fresh with a lustrous finish, and you enjoy styling your hair with waves, sometimes adding one braid to complete the look.

Preppy & Nautical

This Elegant Style Personality is ideal for the lady enchanted with the Classic & Timeless Elegant Style Personality but who prefers every outfit to have an added playful twist! Patterns you can't live without include plaid, polka dots, stripes, and animal prints, and you always wear at least two patterns in every outfit. Your shoe collection is pretty extensive, featuring loafers, oxfords, boat shoes, jeweled sandals, and pumps. Your makeup always coordinates with the colors in your outfit, so if you wear a fuchsia tweed pencil skirt, your lipstick matches it perfectly.

CURATING YOUR WARDROBE

Once you select your Elegant Style Personality, you can create a wardrobe that reflects you with authenticity. All too often, women don't plan ahead for their style and miss the opportunity to use style as a superpower, influencing how others perceive them. You can control not only your reputation, as we explored earlier in this book, but you can control the perception others have of you, too. You have *all* the power; isn't that spectacular?!

Your wardrobe should be thoughtfully developed so that every garment and accessory accurately reflects your Elegant Style Personality. As you shop to supplement your closet, ask yourself before making any purchase: "Is this my Elegant Style Personality _____?" Think about the word you chose to define your Elegant Style Personality. Develop your wardrobe with intention, so that each item you wear is directly aligned with your Elegant Style Personality.

Based on the Elegant Style Personality you chose, you will likely be purchasing different types of items that are the best fit for your specific personal style. The elements of clothing and accessories that differ for each Elegant Style Personality type include various colors, fabrics, and silhouettes.

The colors of the items in your wardrobe will depend on your Elegant Style Personality. For example, the Bold & Edgy Elegant Style Personality includes items in bright colors, while the Classic & Timeless Elegant Style Personality includes items in neutral colors.

The fabrics of the items in your wardrobe will depend on your Elegant Style Personality as well. For example, the perfect jacket for the Bold & Edgy Elegant Style Personality is a leather jacket, while the perfect jacket for the Classic & Timeless Elegant Style Personality is a blazer.

The silhouettes of the items in your wardrobe will also depend on your Elegant Style Personality. For example, the Bold & Edgy Elegant Style Personality includes a mix of loose and structured garments, while the Classic & Timeless Elegant Style Personality includes mostly structured clothes.

On the following pages you will find a guideline for each Elegant Style Personality type with suggested garments, accessories and makeup.

Each Elegant Style Personality listed here can be elegantly coordinated to create a chic and polished appearance. To add an extra touch of class to any Elegant Style Personality, you can coordinate an outfit to include at least one garment from the Classic & Timeless Elegant Style Personality to balance your look with added chic flair.

JE NE SAIS QUOI

Relaxed & Casual Style Guidelines

Tops	Bottoms	Shoes	Colors & Fabric
T-shirts Button-up Shirts Denim Jackets Cotton Dresses	Chino Pants Dress Pants Denim Jeans Cotton Skirts	Non-athletic Sneakers Flip flops Ballet flats	Solid Colors A Few Patterns
Example Outfit: Denim Jeans, a T-shirt, Sneakers, and Mascara with no other makeup.			

Bold & Edgy Style Guidelines

Clothing	Shoes	Makeup	Colors & Fabrics
Black Jeans Jumpsuits T-shirts Vests & Jackets Trendy Clothing Pieces	Platform Boots Ankle Boots Thigh-high Boots High Top Sneakers Pointy Toe Pumps	Well-defined Eyeliner Darker Eyeshadow Darker Lipstick Darker Blush Dramatic Eyelashes	Bright Colors Dark Colors Leather Fabrics Animal Prints
Example Outfit: Black Leather Skirt, Rolling Stones T-shirt, Ankle Boots, Leopard Print Clutch Handbag, Black Eyeliner, Mauve Lipstick, and Dark Blush.			

Simple & Minimalist Style Guidelines

Clothing	Shoes	Jewelry	Makeup	Colors
Dark Wash Jeans Dress Pants Chino Pants Cardigans Blazers Blouses T-shirts Button-up Shirts Pencil Skirts	Loafers Ballet Flats Pumps	One type of metal in each outfit (All yellow gold or all silver)	Natural colors for all makeup products • Eyeshadow • Mascara • Lipstick • Blush	Solid Colors Neutral Colored Clothing (Black, White, Camel, Navy, and Gray)
Example Outfit: a White Button-up Shirt with Dark Wash Denim Jeans, Loafers, a Yellow Gold Bracelet, a Black Leather Tote Bag, Makeup done with Earth-toned Eyeshadow and a Natural Lipstick Color, along with Light Blush.				

Romantic & Feminine Style Guidelines

Clothing	Shoes	Makeup	Colors, Fabrics & Prints
Silk Blouses Cardigans Sweaters Dresses Skirts	Ballet Flats Pumps Jeweled Sandals	Soft colors for all makeup products • Eyeshadow • Lipstick • Blush	Pastel Colored Clothing (Lots of Shades of Pink, Red, Cream and White) Lace Fabrics Silk Fabrics Floral Prints
Example Outfit: a Pink Floral Skirt, a Silk Blouse, Heels, and Makeup applied with Light Pink Lipstick and Light Blush.			

Classic & Timeless Style Guidelines

Clothing	Shoes	Jewelry	Makeup	Colors & Patterns
Trench Coats Blouses Button-up Shirts Dark Wash Jeans Dress Pants Chino Pants A-line Dresses Sheath Dresses Pencil Skirts Cardigans Blazers Neck Scarves	Loafers Ballet Flats Pumps	Pearl Necklaces Pearl Earrings Coordinated jewelry to match every outfit with at least two pieces	Natural colors for all makeup products • Eyeshadow • Mascara • Lipstick • Blush	Neutral Colored Clothing (Black, White, Camel, Navy, and Gray) Stripe Patterns

Example Outfit: a Silk blouse, a Pencil Skirt, a Tweed Blazer, Heels, a Pearl Necklace, a Cream Satchel Handbag and Makeup done with Earth-Toned Eyeshadow, Light Blush, and Red Lipstick.

Boho & Whimsical Style Guidelines

Clothing	Shoes	Jewelry	Makeup	Colors & Patterns
60's & 70's Inspired Pieces Maxi Dresses Maxi Skirts Knit Sweaters Wide-Leg Pants Kimonos	Leather Sandals Clogs Ankle Booties Woven Mules Leather Slides Slingback Heels Espadrille Sandals	Pendant Necklaces Fringe Earrings Earth Stone Jewelry	Dark, Earth-Tone Eyeshadow Colors Pink Lipstick Red Lipstick	Earth-Tone Colors Bright Colors Pastel Colors Floral Patterns

Example Outfit: a Tank Top, a Maxi Skirt in Floral Print, Leather Sandals, a Long Pendant Necklace, Brown Leather Hobo Handbag, Makeup with Dark Brown Eyeshadow and Light Pink Lipstick.

JE NE SAIS QUOI

Preppy & Nautical Style Guidelines

Clothing	Shoes	Jewelry	Makeup	Colors & Patterns
Vests Blazers Cardigans Cable Sweaters Button-up Shirts Blouses Dark Wash Jeans Chino Pants A-line Dresses Sheath Dresses Pleated Skirts	Oxford Shoes Loafers Ballet Flats Pumps	Pearl Necklaces Pearl Earrings Fringe Earrings Jewelry is Mixed and Matched with Various Metals and Colors	Natural colors for makeup products • Eyeshadow • Mascara • Blush Lipstick Color Coordinates with Outfit	Nautical Colors (Navy, Red and White) Leopard Patterns Stripe Patterns Geometric Patterns Plaid Patterns Multiple Patterns in One Outfit
Example Outfit: Plaid Button-up Shirt, Quilted Vest, Candy-Pink Chino Pants, Striped Loafers, Navy Crossbody Handbag, and Makeup with Earth-Toned Eyeshadow, Light Blush, and Candy-Pink Lipstick.				

THE IMPORTANCE OF FIT

As you expand your wardrobe, keep in mind that everything you own should fit you properly. Clothing is meant to flatter you, and it must fit you properly to do that. The quality of your appearance is based more on the fit of your clothing than the caliber of the fabric. Clothing should not be too loose and baggy or too tight and fitted. As an example, a $10 pair of dress pants that fit you properly will compliment you better than a $100 pair of dress pants that are too big and sag on your hips.

It is very rare to find clothing from department stores consistently that will fit you perfectly right off the rack. As an alternative to discovering items with the perfect fit, you can create them. The best way to ensure your clothing properly fits your body is to purchase an item in a size that properly fits the largest area of your body. This allows garments to have extra room to get tailored by an alteration professional. Tailoring your clothing will make sure that you have the proper fit for each garment you wear.

Clothing should fit you to flatter you.

Tailoring your clothing is a worthwhile investment. Wearing clothing that fits you properly not only helps you to feel more comfortable, but you'll feel more confident, too! Clothing that fits you incorrectly says "frumpy" if it's too big and "risqué" if it's too small. I highly doubt that the Elegant Style Personality word you chose was "frumpy" or "risqué." Instead of 20 dresses that fit you somewhat okay, two dresses that look exquisite on you make for a better wardrobe. A wardrobe with je ne sais quoi focuses on quality, not quantity.

WARDROBE ESSENTIALS

Regardless of your Elegant Style Personality type, there are a few essential items that every elegant woman needs for a complete wardrobe. Every elegant wardrobe includes essential pieces that are functional for a variety of personal and professional occasions, which are important because of the versatility you'll have from each piece.

Among the list of elegant wardrobe essentials includes:

- A black dress

- A trench coat

- A white button-up or blouse pullover shirt

- A black, navy, or gray suit (can consist of pants, a skirt, or a dress)

- A pair of closed-toe black pumps

- A pair of white non-athletic sneakers

- A solid color clutch handbag

JE NE SAIS QUOI

A little black dress can be worn to the office for a day of work, a restaurant for a dinner date, to a friend's home for a dinner party, or a professional event for networking. That one piece in your wardrobe, a black dress, is tasteful and can be paired appropriately with different accessories to create the perfect look for a variety of events or occasions.

Essential items are a worthwhile investment for your wardrobe and should be purchased with a focus on quality, not quantity, so that you can get the most usage from each piece. Buying a more expensive black dress from Neiman Marcus that you can wear for five years is worth every penny compared to a cheap black dress from Walmart that you can wear for only five days before you have to replace it again.

When investing in wardrobe essentials, spend time browsing the available inventory at a variety of stores so you can find the best items just for you. There is no need to rush when creating or updating your wardrobe. Taking your time ensures you buy only items you truly love instead of the first blouse or clutch bag that catches your eye at Nordstrom.

> *Building a wardrobe is better done right than done rushed.*

When you buy items that you don't love but merely like or think are "nice," you are wasting money. Buying items that you don't love is a waste of money because you'll rarely wear them. You won't wear clothing and accessories that are merely "nice" as often as the pieces you truly love. Purchasing clothing and accessories is for the purpose of wearing them, not having them hanging up for display in your walk-in closet. Instead, focus on spending the time necessary to build your perfect wardrobe full of items that you love and will enjoy wearing.

CREATING YOUR SIGNATURE LOOK

Now that you have established your Elegant Style Personality, you have the one word that describes how you want others to perceive you based on your appearance. And you know to make sure everything you own is tailored for the proper fit. You also have the list of wardrobe essentials to add to your collection of clothing and accessories. As we continue refining your personal style, let's develop your signature look.

Your signature look allows people to expect how you show up to be consistent, and creates the visual representation of your personal brand. Choosing your signature piece is an art. You should select a piece of clothing, color, accessory, or beauty product that makes you feel confident and powerful! Your signature piece is what makes your signature look work, so selecting something that you enjoy regularly wearing is important.

The key to a signature style piece is that it is something you keep consistent in your outfit and wear every day. You can select a specific piece of clothing, a clothing detail, a particular piece of jewelry, a type of accessory, a color, a hairstyle, or a makeup product for your signature piece. For example, a clothing item that could be a signature style piece is a silk scarf, so you would wear different colors and patterns of scarves to coordinate with all your outfits. A color that could be a signature style piece is the color red, so you always wear something red in every outfit, whether it's a blouse, fedora hat, or stunning shade of lipstick.

A clothing detail that could be a signature style piece is fringe, so you reach for fringe leather boots or a suede jacket with fringe to add a dash of fringe in all your looks. Another example is that you could wear a blazer in every outfit to work. That makes a blazer your signature piece. If you wear your hair styled in a chignon with every outfit, that makes the chignon hairstyle your signature piece. Lastly, if you wear silver jewelry with every outfit, selecting different silver necklaces, rings, bracelets, and earrings to coordinate with your ensembles every day, then the metal of silver is your signature piece.

If you are unsure of what signature piece to select for your style, think about what area of your body that you like to accentuate. If you wish to emphasize your collarbone, a silk scarf would be a perfect signature piece for you! If you like to highlight your legs, pencil skirts would be an ideal choice for your signature piece! If you wish to accentuate your cheeks, perhaps a lovely shade of blush is your perfect signature piece!

Whatever you decide to select for your signature piece, you can create your signature look by wearing it with every outfit. Your signature look should be tasteful and authentic, just like your Elegant Style Personality.

Style is a tool for communication and an enjoyable way to express yourself. You can take pleasure in getting dressed to show people who you are by carefully selecting the clothing and accessories in your wardrobe and signature look. The real power of personal style lies in the fact that you are intentional with what you buy and wear. Being deliberate with your personal style allows you to use the power of it to your advantage.

THE ANNUAL STYLE REVIEW

An annual review of your wardrobe and style ensures that your image is in alignment and authentic to represent how you want to be perceived and the woman you currently are. Everything should be in alignment: your Elegant Style Personality, your signature look, and your wardrobe. Every year, I recommend you revisit the Actionable Advice sections of this chapter. Write a list of personality traits and Elegant Style Personality traits that define who you are, then choose one word to determine your personality and Elegant Style Personality. Also, inventory your wardrobe to ensure that each garment currently fits you properly. If you change words to redefine your Elegant Style Personality or find that clothing fits you looser or tighter than it previously did, then it is time to make some changes and update your wardrobe to reflect your Elegant Style Personality accordingly.

CARING FOR YOUR WARDROBE

As you purchase clothing and accessories to build your wardrobe and continue developing your personal style, the maintenance of your clothing becomes a priority. Wardrobe maintenance includes washing and storing clothing properly. The manner in which you clean and store each piece in your wardrobe affects its longevity, so it's best to care for each and every garment carefully instead of throwing everything you own into the washing machine on a hot water cycle and drying it on high heat.

When washing clothes, follow the recommendations on the clothing label for each garment. Following the garment care recommendations will ensure the integrity of your clothing so you can keep each item looking its best. For example, if a wool car coat has a label that says, "Dry Clean Only," take it to the cleaners instead of tossing it in the washing machine. When ironing clothing garments, use the heat setting based on the highest amount of fabric in the garment. For example, on a blouse with a fabric label containing 80% rayon and 20% polyester, use the iron's heat setting for rayon instead of polyester. Using the appropriate heat setting on the iron ensures that the clothing will not be damaged or burned. Clothing items have been laid to eternal rest because they were damaged by a far-too-hot iron. You can avoid discarding damaged clothing pieces by being mindful of how you wash and iron each garment.

    Properly storing clothes and accessories is another part of wardrobe care. Even when you're rushing in the morning, frantically trying on different clothes to coordinate the perfect outfit for your day, never leave your closet looking like a disaster. The best way to store garments is by zipping up every zipper and buttoning every button before hanging each piece on a hanger or folding it for a drawer. Have you ever tried to put on a dress or jacket you can't wait to wear, and just as you slip it on, the zipper gets stuck and won't budge? That is the worst feeling! Zippers are more likely to get stuck if they haven't been maintained properly. As the seasons in a year change, the clothing you wear each season will change. To make certain that you can wear all the garments that you own throughout the year, it's best to safely store all clothing in a cool, dry place during the months you aren't wearing each piece, with zippers and buttons fastened.

Garment bags are essential wardrobe maintenance items to maintain the quality of your clothing. They protect coats, suits, and formal dresses in your closet. Certain fabrics, such as cashmere and wool, are also great pieces to keep safe in garment bags. Fabric that is taken care of properly looks better for a longer length of time compared to fabric that is carelessly tossed around when washed and stored. When you wear garments that are maintained well, you can enjoy wearing them for years to come.

THE POWER OF YOUR PERSONAL STYLE

Personal style is something that should be personal to you. Your wardrobe, Elegant Style Personality, and signature look should all reflect who you are. Authenticity is crucial so that you can effectively show who you are to others while embracing yourself, fully owning your personal power. A woman with a strong sense of self is a confident woman. A well-dressed woman is a confident and classy woman.

JE NE SAIS QUOI

Expressing your personality is easily achieved with your personal style. Use intention to make sure that each detail, from your Elegant Style Personality to your signature look, accurately reflects who you are as a woman. What you wear influences how others perceive you, and you get to choose what they see. You have the choice to decide what to wear every single day. Let your wardrobe work for you to communicate who you are to the world by always setting intention with what you wear. And whether you love wearing dresses or pants, heels or sneakers, you can carry yourself with class, style, and je ne sais quoi!

Chic Style Secrets

- Wear respectable clothing by keeping your midriff, bosom, and derrière covered.

- Choose tasteful clothing to dress for every occasion appropriately.

- Be authentic in wearing clothing that controls the perception others will have of you so that you showcase your sparkling personality and stay true to who you are.

- Build your wardrobe with items from your Elegant Style Personality, focusing on quality, not quantity.

- Consistently wear one item of clothing, a clothing detail, or a color every day to create your signature look.

- Properly care for each of your garments by following the care recommendations for washing and the fabric contents for ironing.

- Review your personal style once a year to ensure it is an accurate reflection of the woman you currently are. Keep your wardrobe always flattering and polished by making sure all your clothes fit your current body frame well.

CHAPTER 5

BEAUTY ROUTINE

*Outer beauty attracts,
but inner beauty captivates.*

Kate Angell

It's 9 AM, and you are running late for a 9:30 appointment. You have ten minutes to finish getting ready before you head out the door. Instead of coordinating the perfect outfit, styling your hair, and applying makeup, you grab the first blouse and pair of pants within arm's reach from your closet, and, in a mad dash, find your camel cashmere coat as you frantically search between the couch cushions and in various kitchen drawers, for your car keys.

Have you ever had a morning like that? The truth is, when you are short on time, the first thing you sacrifice is your appearance, namely, your beauty routine. A life with je ne sais quoi includes making self-care a priority in order to be beautiful and sparkle by sharing your best, chic self with the world. When you look good on the outside, you feel good on the inside, and others around you are sure to take notice of your compelling elegance!

Self-care is crucial for you, both inside and out. When you honor your body and take care of it by regularly indulging in personal grooming and a beauty routine, you will look and feel your best – with je ne sais quoi! Without a regular beauty routine, you may notice that you don't look or feel as good as you would with a regimen in place.

Your beauty routine isn't exclusively for your benefit. In the moments that matter, like when making a first impression with someone you meet for the first time, your beauty routine will influence how others perceive you. A well-groomed woman is presumed to be confident, organized, and trustworthy. A woman that is not well-groomed is presumed to be apathetic, sloppy, and lazy. Do you want to enter every room confidently with grace and style? Are you hoping to attain the promotion at work? Do you want to start dating to end up with the gentleman of your dreams? Enhancing your appearance can help.

Every woman has a particular preference for her perfect beauty routine. You may enjoy an intensive daily routine and a brief monthly routine. Or you may prefer an intense bi-weekly routine and a brief daily routine. Regardless of how frequently you complete a beauty routine, you should definitely have one.

Your appearance always leaves an impression.

In a world where the average attention span is less than four seconds, there's little time to make an impressive impression, and yet, after every encounter with someone, you are sure to leave them with a lasting thought about you. People will either have a positive or negative impression about you in an instant, so your goal is to make every impression positive and memorable.

With a proper beauty routine, you can take your appearance from average to amazing. It's the start to ensuring you are stunning from head to toe, inside and out!

Let me be clear—when I refer to making enhancements to your appearance, I am specifically suggesting personal grooming and beauty techniques. I am not at all, suggesting plastic surgery or bodily injections in order to help you make better impressions with people. I know that those are options, but those are not options that I endorse.

THE ESSENCE OF YOUR BEAUTY ROUTINE

The essence of a beauty routine is to maintain your personal hygiene and grooming in order to ensure your appearance is clean and well-kept. Daily hygiene practices keep your body clean and healthy for yourself and other people around you. Proper hygiene includes daily bathing of your body, daily brushing and flossing of your teeth, hair removal when necessary, and using the appropriate personal products (deodorant, sunscreen, lotion, and feminine necessities) to maintain your appearance.

Smart hygiene practices are the foundation of a good beauty routine.

When you hear the words, "beauty routine," what first comes to mind? You may think of cosmetic or hair products, which are indeed part of a beauty routine, but at the very core of a good beauty routine is hygiene. Before enhancing your naturally beautiful features, it is important to keep them clean and healthy because healthy skin, hair, and nails radiate beauty from within. Piling on foundation, lipstick, and hairspray is a complete waste of time, money, and effort if you are putting it on dirty skin or oily hair.

The way you take care of yourself day-to-day ultimately determines if you look your best, which leads to you feeling your best. It starts from the inside out. Being healthy is beautiful. When you have a good regular hygiene routine, you will have a good beauty routine.

Some days you may feel like you have no time for a beauty routine. It can be very tempting to cut corners, especially when you have a never-ending to-do list. You might feel pressured to eliminate your beauty routine in order to handle your schedule and increasingly packed calendar. However, your basic hygiene is not something to compromise. After all, you need to feel your best to sparkle and shine when attending all your meetings, appointments, presentations, mixers, and parties. And you'll feel so much more capable if you feel comfortable, clean, and cared for. Quite frankly, hygiene is *never* something you should willingly compromise.

Daily bathing is essential (especially if you exercise regularly) to wash away the toxins your body naturally secretes. Be aware of and address body odor, which is a natural circumstance and never a shameful one. Hygiene also involves addressing body hair in accordance with your preferences, be it hair removal cream, waxing, or shaving. Good basic hygiene mandates that you care for your teeth with daily brushing and flossing (and the strategic use of breath mints when necessary!), as well as regular visits to your doctor and dentist. Your hygiene has implications for your attire and physical presentation. A clean face and body are necessities, especially when it comes to feeling fresh and looking elegant.

YOUR HAIR IS YOUR CROWN

Hair care is an integral part of your beauty routine because your hair is your head's natural crown.

Proper hair maintenance keeps your hair healthy, luscious, and vibrant. Your ideal hair maintenance routine will depend on the type of hair you have. Some women wash their hair twice a day; others wash their hair once a week. At the very least, washing your hair once a week helps you to remove the bacteria, dirt, and oils that build up in your scalp. Whether or not you regularly exercise, you do naturally sweat. More sweat is created during exercise activity, but natural sweat does occur without putting forth significant effort. Sweat leads to bacteria and dirt in your scalp, which is why washing your hair on a regular basis is important.

All hair types and lengths need daily attention. From brushing to combing to wrapping to curling to teasing, you decide how to maintain and style your hair. However, you need to do something to your hair every day for it to look its best. Whether you like to wear your hair wavy, straight, curly, braided, or dreadlocked, your hair's everyday style should be neat and well-kept. Keeping your hair looking elegant means every strand has a proper place, regardless of how you choose to style the texture of your hair. In the evening, you probably have a nightly beauty routine that includes fixing your hair to prepare it for the next day ahead. In the morning, your beauty routine should consist of a few minutes (as many as necessary) to style your hair for the day.

Regular end trims are also necessary for hair maintenance. A swift trim of the ends every six to eight weeks is the typically recommended time frame for getting your hair ends clipped, which will minimize split ends and breakage. If you aren't a hair care professional yourself, it's best to visit one for end-trimming service to maintain the elegant haircut and style of your hair.

THE PERFECT HAIR CARE PRODUCTS

Finding the perfect hair care products is often as difficult as finding the perfect pair of pumps! Every woman's hair is different, so you won't ever know if a product will work well for your hair until you try it. You may have to experiment with various products and brands to create the ideal set of hair care products to wash, nourish, and style your hair, but the adventure is well worth the reward of luscious locks.

If you are in search of hair care products that will make your hair look its best, you can purchase trial sizes of different brands and types of products to find the combination that will work best for you. Another way to fast-track your hair care product collection is to find out what products your hair stylist uses and recommends for your hair type. A variety of shampoos, conditioners, oils, serums, masques, foams, sprays, and moisturizers is typically the best combination. Ultimately, you will have to discover which products and brands your hair will cherish the most.

THE IMPORTANCE OF SKIN CARE

Skin care is often the most significant area women overlook in a comprehensive beauty routine. Healthy skin is beautiful skin. Before spending a considerable amount of money on cosmetic products, taking proper care of your skin first is the priority, and you can do that with excellent products and proper skin care techniques.

THE PERFECT SKIN CARE PRODUCTS

At the heart of a good skin care routine is using the proper products for your skin type. Oily skin requires products with a certain set of ingredients, while dry skin requires a different set of products with different ingredients. If you are unsure of what type of skin you have or what set of ingredients your skin needs, it is a good idea to pay a visit to a dermatologist to find out from a skin care professional.

Similar to hair care products, finding the perfect skin care products for your beauty routine may take some time. Dermatologists don't recommend using an extensive list of products; instead, less is more. Finding your ideal set of products is best achieved by experimenting with a different combination of products until you decide on the perfect combination just for you.

Healthy skin is happy skin.

Actionable Advice

Make an appointment with a dermatologist to inquire about what skin type you have, and the types of products to look for and avoid.

After your session with a skin care professional, visit your bathroom cabinet to review what you currently have based on their recommendations. If you are missing a cleanser, toner, moisturizer, serum, facial mask, or oil, you can search for the proper products for your skin type using the advice from the dermatologist. Once you purchase new products, you may have to apply them in various combinations to determine what works best for your face.

As you experiment with different products, try switching just one product at a time in your routine so you can monitor how your skin reacts to each new product. Adding or removing five new products from or into your beauty routine at once makes it difficult to determine which one made the difference in your skin's health and happiness.

* * * * *

PROPER SKIN MAINTENANCE & PROTECTION

Daily moisturization is also vital for healthy skin. In your skin care routine, you should use a moisturizer in the morning and the evening. You may even want to have two different moisturizers: one for the morning, and one for the evening, based on your skin type. Moisturization throughout the year is also important. As the season changes, your moisturizer should change as well to accommodate the climate. The weather inflicts harsh conditions on our skin (both humidity and heat in the summer and dry coolness in the winter), so your moisturizer can help to protect your skin as the seasons change.

Another important element of a proper beauty routine is exfoliating to keep your skin radiating with a natural glow. Regular exfoliation maintains the health of the skin on your face and body. Dead skin cells shouldn't linger on your body; instead, they should be removed. Exfoliating two to four times a week on your face and body will remove the dead skin cells, so they don't hang around longer than needed.

Sunscreen should also be worn every day. Regardless of the weather or the season, sunscreen should be used to protect your skin from strong sun rays. Whether the day is filled with bright sunshine or is overcast with clouds, your skin still needs UV protection. Every time you leave your home, you are prone to UV exposure. To simplify your skin care routine and streamline your collection of essential beauty products, purchase a moisturizer or cosmetic product, such as foundation primer, that contains sunscreen, so you can wear proper UV protection every day.

Healthy facial skin is rarely touched. In general, touching your face throughout the day is not recommended because picking at your face will likely result in aggravating and irritating your skin. Everyday your hands touch anything and everything under the sun, from doorknobs to light switches to drawer handles. The bacteria on your hands can lead to breakouts, scarring, and even wrinkles after being transferred to your face.

Instead of spreading your hands over your face as a nervous habit, do your best to keep your hands off your face throughout the day, unless you are touching up your makeup or applying cosmetics in the restroom. On any occasion, day or night, the ideal time to touch your face is after washing your hands with soap and water.

Silk pillowcases are a blessing for both your face and hair. The silk helps prevent creasing and wrinkles on your skin and also avoids creating tangles and breakage in your hair. As such, clean silk pillowcases are best to sleep on for a good night's rest to keep your skin and hair healthy!

ELEGANT MAKEUP RULES

Selecting the ideal elegant makeup look is purely a matter of preference. You can decide what products and how many to wear to always look chic and polished. Some women feel they need to wear a full face of makeup daily while others don't. Truthfully, when it comes to whether or not you should wear makeup as a daily look, it's completely up to you, although there are times when its best to wear makeup, even if it's just for special occasions, like formal evening events or professional headshot photos.

You wear the makeup; it shouldn't wear you.

The one elegant makeup rule of thumb is this: pick one feature of your face to highlight at a time. If you want to feature your lips, you will likely want to wear a darker shade of lip color while keeping other makeup colors more natural. If you want to feature your eyes, you will likely want to wear a darker eyeliner or eyeshadow color while maintaining a softer look on the rest of your face.

ELEGANT MAKEUP APPLICATION

The best course of action to take for applying makeup is to think about how you want to look and how much time you want to spend achieving that look on a regular basis. Whether you prefer a two-product or ten-product makeup regimen, it's best to keep your look consistent, at least for the office and running errands around town. You will probably want to change up your makeup look for evening affairs, such as cocktail parties, date nights, and charity galas.

Makeup products that complement your skin tone and are applied correctly will only ever elevate your entire appearance.

Always apply makeup on fresh, clean skin. When building your makeup collection, reach for products that complement your skin tone and natural features.

Earth tones are generally a good choice for eye colors, including eyeshadow and eyeliner. If your skin tone has a warm undertone, shades of green, brown, and gold will be the best color choices to enhance your natural beauty. If your skin tone has a cool undertone, shades of blue, gray, and silver will be the best color choices to enhance your natural beauty.

CREATING YOUR ELEGANT EVERYDAY MAKEUP LOOK

When creating your elegant everyday makeup look, you can be thoughtful in the products you wear to always put your best face forward.

Below are a few time-tested tips to apply makeup with class:

- Select one area of your face to feature—eyes, lips, or cheeks.

- For an elegant and polished look, wearing natural colors for makeup is recommended. Look chic by avoiding neon colors for lips, cheeks, and eyes (unless you are attending a costume party).

- Wear foundation that matches your skin tone and eyebrow gel, powder or pencil that matches your natural eyebrow color.

- Reach for complementary eyeshadow and eyeliner colors based on your skin's undertones.

- If you don't want to do a full face of makeup, opt for a simple look, including eyeshadow, eyeliner, mascara, foundation, blush, and lip color.

- False eyelashes with a natural length and volume are classy for an everyday look. Long, full eyelashes give your eyes more drama and are best reserved for special occasions, such as photo shoots, charity galas, cocktail parties, and date nights.

- If you know you don't like wearing makeup every day, save it for special occasions, like photo shoots, charity galas, cocktail parties, and date nights.

BECOMING COMFORTABLE WITH MAKEUP

Many women are never formally taught makeup techniques. If you don't know the difference between an eyelash curler and an eyelash comb, you are not alone. You can always learn about makeup products and techniques.

It is never too late to enhance your elegant self!

Actionable Advice

If the world of makeup feels foreign to you, don't fret!

Take some time to experiment with wearing makeup every day, before investing a significant amount into products, tools, and applicators, to determine how you feel and if you enjoy the daily routine of application and removal.

Make a trip to a local department or beauty store and ask a beauty professional what products and colors will work best for you. A second opinion is especially helpful to make sure your foundation is just the right shade to match your skin.

After you've purchased a few cosmetic products, you're ready to start your experiment over a 14-day trial period. Spend two weeks wearing makeup every day, with as many or as few products as you like but which all complement your natural features and skin's undertones. In your journal, write down how it makes you feel wearing makeup.

You may enjoy the extra boost of confidence makeup gives you or the compliments from others about your appearance, or you may not like spending an additional 15 minutes or more every morning in the bathroom mirror. Monitor how you feel wearing daily makeup, and write down your reflections in your journal.

After the two weeks, you can decide what your everyday makeup routine should be. You can determine your plan for makeup based on how you felt during your experiment. Feeling more graceful and beautiful with makeup may encourage you to wear makeup daily if wearing it is new to you. Not noticing an improvement in how you feel, feeling self-conscious, or feeling worse about your appearance with makeup applied may discourage you from wearing makeup daily.

The notes in your journal and feelings in your heart should be your deciding factor on whether or not you want to pursue wearing makeup every day as a new addition to your daily beauty routine.

* * * * *

THE PERFECT COSMETIC PRODUCTS

Discovering the perfect brands for cosmetic products is another elegant journey to creating your life with je ne sais quoi (if you choose to wear makeup every day). It's one to both embrace and enjoy for the ride! The perfect makeup products in your beauty routine shouldn't break out your skin or cause irritation or scarring. Makeup sets and trial sizes are a smart way to cost-effectively try various products and colors to test them out at home.

When shopping, another alternative for finding the best makeup products and colors to keep you looking chic is to try out products at beauty counters in department stores by swiping colors on the back of your hand. Regardless of how you choose to find and experiment with cosmetics, give yourself some grace as you patiently explore the world of beauty to pinpoint the best products for your beauty routine.

Actionable Advice

Whether you are new to makeup or a beauty maven, if you choose to wear makeup every day, write down in your journal the details of your darling daily look.

A consistent makeup look for leaving home to go to work, run errands, and fulfill your social calendar will keep you looking polished and graceful at all times.

* * * * *

ELEGANT NAILCARE
& HAND MAINTENANCE

Nails are a wonderful way to express your personality. Healthy nails will radiate with beauty, just like your hair, skin, and face. Keeping your nails looking gorgeous will enhance your overall elegant appearance.

Whether you decide to keep them polished or buffed, always strive to keep your nails looking beautiful. Regular nail maintenance ensures your nails will be healthy and happy. A weekly manicure to remove dirt underneath, remove dead skin, care for your cuticles, file, and buff to a shine can be done at either a local nail salon or at home.

> *Nails, like hair, are just another accessory we wear.*

Nail polish should only be worn entirely on or entirely off the nail. If you don't like to wear nail colors, a clear polish or unpolished but buffed nails are perfectly acceptable ways to look well-groomed and pulled together. If you do wear nail polish, it's best to have the full color applied to your whole nail. When the polish starts to chip, remove the nail polish to reveal clean nails or reapply a gorgeous new color. Chipped nail polish is distasteful and never a part of an elegant appearance.

ELEGANT NAIL RULES

The rule for wearing nail colors with elegance is to select a soft, natural color of nail polish. Shades of pink, red, brown, gray, and nude are the most elegant colors to wear. These neutral nail colors will complement instead of clashing with your wardrobe, regardless of what color your dress, pants, blouse, handbag, or shoes may be. Keeping your nails short with a rounded oval or square shape is more elegant than long nails with pointy shapes, like the stiletto, ballerina, or squareletto styles. Elegant nails are meant to be dainty and feminine, not to rival the claws of a grizzly bear!

ELEGANT HAND CARE

Hands are best taken care of with products made just for them! Hand cream nourishes while replenishing with moisture and is perfect for applying after washing your hands, especially during cool winter months. Moisturizing hand gloves are another elegant beauty godsend to keep your hands vibrant and healthy. Beautiful and soft hands, like the hands of bracelet models from Tiffany & Co., are attractive and smooth as silk thanks to hand gloves! Before going to bed at night, you can apply lotion or hand cream before slipping on the gloves. Overnight, while you are sleeping, the gloves will help your hands to absorb essential oils and refresh them to look young and radiant the following morning!

MAINTAINING YOUR EYEBROWS

Last but not least in your beauty routine is eyebrow maintenance. Elegant eyebrows frame your face and make your natural features gleam and glow. A polished look includes defined eyebrows that are shaped without excessive hairs above or below the shape of the brow.

Your eyebrows, like your hair, will grow at their own pace. But it's important to keep an eye on them (pun intended!) to monitor when they need to be kept in check. When hairs grow in between your eyebrows or above or below the defined shape of each one, it is time to get them waxed, plucked, or threaded to remove those scraggly hairs. You can choose to maintain your eyebrows with regular visits to a beauty professional or by doing the deed at home in the mirror; either way, maintaining your eyebrows is a top priority and should never be forgotten.

THE EVOLUTION OF YOUR BEAUTY ROUTINE

Ultimately, your beauty routine will evolve over time. Old products will need to be replaced, and new products will need to be purchased to keep up with the circle of life your body experiences. This is just part of living and maturing with elegance. Typically, your skin care and hair care products will need to be upgraded with each new decade, so as you age into a new era, consider reviewing the products you use in order to keep yourself looking radiant and beautiful.

Being in touch with your body is critically important to be both healthy and beautiful. You should be aware of the natural ways your skin looks, feels, and smells so that if anything ever changes, you will notice the shift, and go to a doctor for help. Your health is the most important thing you have in life because without it you can't do anything else. A proper beauty routine is not just about looking good. It's about feeling good, and in order to feel amazing, you have to take amazing care of yourself first. Your body is the only one you will ever have, so clean and care for it well, inside and out, to look and feel your best every day.

JE NE SAIS QUOI
Chic Beauty Secrets

- A life with je ne sais quoi includes both inner and outer beauty.

- Beauty professionals are a wealth of knowledge and can help you figure out what skin care, hair care, and cosmetic products will work best for you.

- Visit a dermatologist to determine what skin type you have and get product recommendations.

- Ask your hair stylist for hair product recommendations for your hair type.

- Visit a department store or beauty professional yearly for help to match your foundation.

- Keep your makeup routine elegant by choosing one feature of your face to highlight in each makeup look.

- Wear makeup colors that complement you, based on your skin's undertone.

- Keep your nails elegant with soft, natural colors, short length, and round or square shape.

- Maintain your eyebrows by removing scraggly hairs above and below your natural brow.

- Review your beauty routine and products with each new decade you enjoy, to keep your chic self elegant as you evolve.

CHAPTER 6

HEALTHY HABITS

It is health that is real wealth, not pieces of gold and silver.

Mahatma Gandhi

Think of all the things you do in an average week: going to work, taking your children to activities, attending social events, running errands, and cooking meals. Your to-do list never ends—would you be able to do *all* the things you typically do if you were under the weather? When you don't have good health, everything else in your life is consequently far more difficult and challenging.

There's no doubt that a life with je ne sais quoi includes self-care and healthy habits. From appointments to meetings to events to errands, you spend a lot of time, energy, and effort on other people and priorities. It's also important to make yourself a priority. You have to take care of yourself first to then take care of others effectively. You should be the top priority on your list by making sure you get the food, vitamins, exercise, sleep, water, and relaxation that you need. Without taking care of your body, both inside and out, you won't be able to do the things you need to do for your family, friends, or co-workers.

When you take optimal care of yourself, you will feel the difference. After a good night's rest, you will have more energy throughout the day. After a workout, you will have an extra bounce in your step. After drinking a gallon (or two) of water, you will be greeted in the mirror by clearer, brighter skin.

The benefits of a healthy lifestyle are endless, and the best part about the benefits of good health is that for many of them, you will both see and feel a significant enhancement! The healthy habits you live by can easily be enforced after thoughtfully crafting a routine with activities for a healthy lifestyle. Fortunately for you, healthy habits are easy to maintain once you establish them.

CREATING NEW, HEALTHY HABITS

The key to living with long-term elegance is first to be aware of your behavior by identifying what your current habits are, then applying the principles and techniques in this book to take your chic life to the next level. The more frequently you apply the principles of elegant living, the more ingrained in your mind they will become. This means that, through repetition, you will have habits that come naturally without having to concentrate very hard to do them.

You also have the incredible power of choice. You can choose to live stressed, depressed, anxious, unhappy, and unfulfilled, or you can choose to live with elegance, confidence, peace, happiness, and fulfillment. No one can choose how you live your life. So, choose how you want to live carefully in order to make the most of the beautiful life that you have.

When establishing new habits, it's best to ease yourself into them for long-term success. For example, upon registering for a 10K marathon to raise funds and awareness for breast cancer research, you will train to get your body in shape for the run. If you haven't exercised in several years, it will be difficult to start running every day. Instead, to train and condition properly, you can spend time daily walking before gradually increasing the time and speed of your walks to create a daily habit of running. Starting this new habit of running will get you in tip-top shape for the 10K!

HEALTHY EATING HABITS

How you feel, look and act are all influenced by your eating habits. The foods you put into your body will either fuel and supercharge you or drain you, depending on what you eat. We all have moments that cravings and temptations prevail, but generally speaking, it is best not to indulge in convenient, comfort foods but in nutritious, nourishing foods.

An energized body will give you the vigor to be your best self at work, at home, and in life. A fatigued body is a distraction from focusing on a task or conversation at hand and motivates you to give less than your best effort. Every meal and snack is a choice that can propel you forward or prevent you from attaining your peak performance.

Consider this: it's 2 PM on a Tuesday. You are experiencing the 'afternoon slump' and are ready for a snack. You have two options: a handful of chocolate chip cookie sandwiches filled with icing, or celery sticks and peanut butter. The chocolate may be calling your name, but this issue is one of mind over matter. Enjoying a delightful snack of cookie sandwiches will send you on a sugar high that will crash by 4 PM. This is the remarkable impact of food and how it can enhance or destruct your entire day! Your mind may crave the cookies while your body yearns for the celery. Being intentional with what you eat for every meal and snack can help you make the smart choice.

In addition to your energy level, what you eat impacts how you look. It's no secret that the foods you habitually eat do contribute to your outer appearance. Foods that are fried, greasy, and processed will not give you a slim waistline or radiant skin. Making smart choices about what you eat can help your body be long, lean, clear, and blemish-free. Your hair and nails will also be healthy and grow faster by making smart food choices.

Healthy foods give you a beautiful glow.

Actionable Advice

In your journal, review your current eating habits with a food audit. At this point, you don't need to make any changes to your food lifestyle. This is just an activity to gain clarity about what you typically eat. We often don't realize the individual food choices we make because as ingrained habits, we cook and eat 'the usual,' without consciously making each decision.

Spend the next 14 days eating what you usually eat. For each day, list the date at the top of a new page in your journal and create a section for each meal you enjoyed. In each meal section, write down the foods, snacks, and beverages you consumed, along with the amount of each item. If you eat once a day, just list out everything you ate for that particular day in your journal. If you skip eating for an entire day, list the date and make a note that you didn't eat.

Below is an example of one recorded meal for inspiration in formatting your two-week food assessment.

<u>Date - December 3</u>
Meal - Lunch (12:30 PM)
3 slices of barbecue chicken pizza
1 bag of salted pretzels
1 glass of fruit punch
1 chocolate chip cookie

There is no need to feel ashamed or embarrassed, and you will be the only person to see this food chronicle unless you decide to share it. This audit is an honest look at your typical food choices to review the type of habits you currently have.

* * * * *

EATING WELL WITH INTENTION

The best foods to support how you feel and look are fruits, vegetables, and all-natural ingredients. When you can, you should do your best to avoid buying processed boxes, cans, bags, and cartons of food to eat.

The more processed a food item is, the less healthy it is for you.

Consider this: fresh vegetables, like spinach and broccoli, are better for you than canned vegetables, like green beans or peas and carrots, because canned foods are loaded with sodium, sugar, and other additives to preserve their ability to be edible. Either fresh or frozen produce are the best choices. Plain yogurt, Greek yogurt, and low-fat yogurt are better dairy choices than flavored yogurt or fat-free yogurt. The healthiest meats to eat are fish, turkey, and chicken instead of red meats, like lamb, pork, and beef. Tofu and plant-based protein sources are great choices for vegetarian and vegan lifestyles, as well.

When food choices are intentional, you give your body the nutrients and nourishment you need to look and feel radiant. Avoiding trans fats, baked goods, processed snacks, and fried foods are the best way to start making simple changes in your lifestyle to see a big difference. Adding more fruits and vegetables, whole grains, ancient grains, and nuts to your plate should help you feel healthier and fuller, too.

One way to save time and stress when it comes to making positive food choices is to plan your meals in advance. During a hectic day, the last thing you need to worry about is where to find a snack because, in a hasty rush, you are likely to rely on convenience. It won't help your health to find yourself driving away from the drive-thru at McDonald's with a cola, hamburger, and salted fries to satisfy your appetite.

Actionable Advice

One day a week, sit down, plan, and write out the meals and snacks you want to have for the week ahead. Then make your grocery list accordingly and shop for the items you'll need. That way, during your busy schedule, you have meals and snacks that are healthy on hand, so you don't have to scramble and decide what you want for every meal and snack throughout the week.

* * * * *

It may take more time to cook wholesome meals, but that time is an investment in your well-being, and it is certainly well worth the hours you'll spend. You can even have a delightful experience with family instead of a burdensome chore by cooking a meal together and making it enjoyable.

UPGRADING YOUR FOOD CHOICES

Review your two-week food audit once the journal entries are complete. If you are open to improving your food habits by selecting healthier food choices, you now have a good idea of where to start based on your current choices. If you decide to make some food changes in your life, taking it one step at a time is an excellent approach for long-term progress. Start by improving food choices for one meal each week, then gradually continue to improve another snack or meal until you have upgraded your complete week of eating to include nutritious foods with a few treats sprinkled in.

A HEALTHY LIFESTYLE
IS ALL ABOUT BALANCE

I don't like the word, "diet," because it refers to shifting eating habits for only a temporary period of time. Instead, I use the phrase, "food lifestyle choices," because truly healthy habits are less about on-and-off again foods, and more about the selections you make on a regular basis. It is acceptable to indulge in a donut now and then, but a donut is not a healthy breakfast for every weekday morning. The best food choices account for a balanced lifestyle, with everything in moderation.

THE NUTRIENTS YOU NEED

A life with je ne sais quoi is about being your best, and you can't function at your highest level if your food choices are vitamin deficient. In addition to eating nutritious foods on a regular basis, vitamins will give you the extra nutrients your body needs to thrive. As women, necessary vitamins including folic acid, calcium, C, and D help to keep our bones, cells, and body healthy and strong.

Whether your lifestyle includes meat or is vegan, a multivitamin is strongly recommended to give you the extra nutrients your body may not be receiving from food. The time of day doesn't much matter when you take vitamins, but it's important to take vitamins every day, just as you brush your teeth or hair. With all the varieties available—capsules, gummies, powder, liquid, and chewables—you can find the type of vitamin that works best for you.

HEALTHY MOVEMENT HABITS

Exercise is another healthy habit to incorporate into your lifestyle. The list of benefits from regularly exercising are endless, but to name a few: weight loss, lowering your risk of numerous diseases, increased energy, improving the health of your skin, and enhancing brain health and memory functioning. All these results contribute to creating your healthy life with je ne sais quoi. It's commonly known from many scientific studies that you can increase the length of your life by regularly exercising.

In combination with a routine of eating healthy foods, regular exercise puts you on track toward living your best life. If you take care of your body, it will take care of you, supporting you with energy and strength to accomplish all your goals and ambitions.

Exercising should move your body and burn calories. Simple, small changes in your regular lifestyle, like parking in the back of the lot at the mall and walking a little farther or taking the stairs instead of the elevator to attend your next meeting, can improve your overall health. Whether you spend your work days sitting or standing, you still need at least 30 minutes of moderate physical activity a few times a week to be healthy. For a healthy lifestyle, the American Heart Association recommends 30 minutes a day of moderate exercise for five days a week or 25 minutes a day of vigorous exercise for three days a week.

You can easily fulfill that recommendation with a variety of activities. You may enjoy moderate exercise, such as walking, hiking, tennis, ballroom dancing, biking less than 10 miles per hour, or water aerobics. Or you may prefer vigorous exercise, such as jogging, running, jumping rope, swimming laps, or biking more than 10 miles per hour. Stretching exercises, like yoga and Pilates, along with weight training exercises with dumbbells or machines are also good additions to your workout routine.

However you choose to exercise, once you start to see and feel the changes from increasing your strength and stamina, you are much more likely to commit to your workout routine for all the long-term benefits.

Actionable Advice

Discover exercise that you enjoy – try something new if your current exercise routine doesn't include something you have fun doing (or if you don't have an exercise activity that you enjoy).

Spend time each week doing one new exercise activity until you find workouts that you look forward to doing!

Once you find exercises that you like, write them in your journal to keep a list of the various ways you can keep your body moving every week to be healthy.

* * * * *

HEALTHY SLEEPING HABITS

You require your body to do a lot during any given day, so it's crucial to provide it with what it needs to help you do all that you need to do. Getting adequate sleep each night impacts your physical, mental, and emotional health. And it's the quickest (and cheapest) way to remove bags from under your eyes! Our bodies function at the highest level throughout the day after a good night of sleep. It's impossible to gracefully navigate your day when you're sleep deprived and irritable.

So, how much rest is enough to look and be your best?

Adult women should strive to sleep at least seven to nine hours each night to live a healthy, alert, and active life. The quality of sleep you have each night can be improved by having a regular schedule for when you sleep and wake up each day. As you get ready for bed each evening, power down electronics at least 60 minutes before you go to sleep and enjoy a relaxing activity, like taking a warm bath or reading a book. Relaxation before bed helps your body to wind down and prepare for rest.

Sleep deprivation has frightening effects on your body. When you don't get enough sleep, you are likely to suffer from decreased focus, memory retention, and mood regulation. Improper rest can also lead to obesity from the lack of appetite control and increase your risk of diabetes and cardiovascular disease.

HEALTHY HYDRATION HABITS

Would an elegant, graceful woman have dry hands, brain fog, or an irritable attitude? Of course not, but those things can happen when you're dehydrated. Proper water intake flushes out toxins from your body, prevents headaches, increases brain power, gives you an energy boost, and promotes healthy weight maintenance and weight loss. Hydration works wonders for your skin, hair, and nails, too. It's one of the best beauty regimen activities because it also benefits your health! When you drink enough water every day, you will experience a better mood, more energy, and an overall higher quality of life.

The old adage of recommending eight glasses of eight ounces of water every day is just that—old. Women should aim to drink between nine and eleven glasses of eight ounces of water every day to be hydrated and healthy. If you feel thirsty, have a dry mouth, or notice dark yellow urine after using the restroom, you are experiencing signs of dehydration.

Drinking water doesn't have to be a daily chore; it can be an enjoyable part of your healthy lifestyle. If plain water doesn't tickle your fancy, you can always add tea leaves, fruits, vegetables, or herbs for flavor. Fresh mint from a local farmer's market or your backyard garden makes a lovely addition to a glass of water. Spa water with cucumber slices doesn't have to be enjoyed exclusively at the spa; you can prepare it at home for a nice treat. Carbonated water is also an option for daily water intake if you prefer your water to sparkle with bubbles decorating the rim of your glass.

HEALTHY RELAXATION HABITS

If you are always on the go, downtime and rest are especially essential to incorporate into your healthy lifestyle. Relaxation is crucial for good health and positively impacts your physical, mental, and emotional well-being. When you relax, you give yourself the gift of disconnecting from responsibility to enjoy being in the moment. You can't give your best effort to one task or activity if you are always going nonstop. Taking a daily pause for rest will rejuvenate your body and mind and give you an extra boost of energy and happiness to conquer everything else in your day.

Relaxation can be defined however you choose, but it should involve an enjoyable activity that doesn't include stress or anxiety. You can do yoga, go for a walk at the park, read a book, bake a cake, knit a hat, draw a sketch, write poetry, paint a picture, take photographs, or even be pampered with a massage or facial to relax. The activity you choose for relaxation is simply a matter of your preference. The point is to pick something you enjoy doing and do it at least a few minutes each day.

Women often take care of everyone and everything else but themselves. I encourage you to start taking care of you. You have one body, one brain, one heart – care for them like you do your children, husband, and parents. Every day spend at least 20 minutes for rest and relaxation (aside from sleeping) to help you to manage the activities and responsibilities in your life effectively.

Actionable Advice

In your journal, write a list of relaxing activities you enjoy that give you the pleasurable gift of unplugging from responsibility.

Make time each evening to do something for at least twenty minutes to relax before turning in for the night and going to bed.

* * * * *

THE POWER OF HABITS

Healthy habits aren't about trying something for a few days or weeks and then stopping. Healthy habits are about creating a lifestyle for you so that you can thrive, being the best woman possible to live your best life. When you don't get enough sleep, water, or eat the right foods, you will undoubtedly feel the difference. Instead of paying the price with an unhealthy life, spend a few minutes creating a healthy lifestyle so that you can have an elegant life and thrive with je ne sais quoi.

Eating healthy foods, exercising regularly, and getting enough sleep and water is a tough combination to accomplish. The truth is, most women fall short of fully committing to a healthy lifestyle. But you don't have to be one of them.

The easiest way to set yourself up for success is to plan ahead so that you make decisions in advance and avoid frantic scrambling in the moment.

Your quality of life lies entirely within your control. You choose what you eat or don't eat, how much you sleep or don't sleep, and if you exercise or don't exercise. You have the choice to live with energy, focus, and good health. It is up to you to select your habits; just be sure you are intentional when doing so. Think carefully about what you are choosing. Be empowered to shape your life in a manner that will have you feeling and looking vibrant.

Chic Health Secrets

- Plan your meals and grocery shop a week in advance, so your food choices are healthy, not hazardous.

- Buy and take vitamins regularly. Purchase a bottle or two at the store once a month or whenever you need to replenish your supply.

- Commit to exercising regularly, engaging in physical activities that you enjoy.

- Prioritize your exercise by adding your workouts to your calendar as part of your schedule.

- Create a sleeping routine by striving to go to bed and wake up at the same times each day.

- Keep a water bottle with you throughout the day so you can make sure you reach your water intake goal. Add fruits, herbs, or tea to keep the flavor interesting.

- Relax every evening before bed, doing an activity you enjoy for at least twenty minutes that doesn't involve an electronic device. This time is non-negotiable and blocked out on your calendar to ensure its priority status.

PART 3
CHARM

CHAPTER 7

COMPELLING CHARACTER

Character, not circumstance, makes the person.

Booker T. Washington

Character is your ability to live elegantly every day, exhibit behavior in good taste and be courteous to others. Your character is difficult to measure and impossible to touch, but it is easily recognized and always sincerely felt by others because your character drives your behavior and interactions.

Your character allows you to operate, say, and do things in accordance with your beliefs and to be thoughtful in your actions instead of being rash. A life with je ne sais quoi includes applying morals and values to your daily life in a way that makes you fascinating and attractive to others. You think before you speak and are careful to be courteous with others at all times.

Actions speak louder than words. Often in life, what you *do* matters more than what you *say*. As the old saying goes, talk is cheap.

As you make decisions throughout the day, it's helpful to rely upon a confirmed set of standards. Particularly in difficult decisions, when you might struggle with deciding how to respond or react during a conflict, a set of standards can guide you to take the best course of action. This is what I call your Decorum Code.

The Decorum Code is a set of values that serve as the standards you live by. The Decorum Code you create for yourself and abide by is personal to you, and it is an authentic expression of your individual values.

In life, you can either stand for something or fall for anything.

The Decorum Code that you create serves as the foundation for every potential decision you make, word you say, or action you take. Your Decorum Code is based on life principles that you select as the most pertinent to you. Instead of personality traits or hobbies, your Decorum Code includes your fundamental beliefs. The Decorum Code is far deeper in meaning and application than a list of personality traits because your beliefs determine who you are and how you live your life. This is your opportunity to make a commitment to yourself regarding how you define your character, the qualities about you that describe the essence of who you are as a woman.

Before establishing your personal Decorum Code, let's explore a variety of core values that you could potentially include. Respect, integrity, honor, compassion, dependability, courage, perseverance, and loyalty are just a few of the endless core values you can incorporate into your Decorum Code. Each value is absolute; you either live according to it or you don't. You can't be somewhat respectful or sometimes courageous – you either treat people with respect or you don't. You either live courageously, or you don't.

ELEGANT CHARACTER VALUES

RESPECT

Respect refers to the belief of consideration, specifically how you consider treating other people and how you consider taking care of yourself. Being considerate of other people means you care about their feelings and overall well-being. Being considerate of yourself means you take care of yourself and are intentional in the way you present yourself around others.

Respect is the most universal language in the world. Respect is given with or without words and is displayed by your actions. What you say and do around people shows them whether or not you respect them. Respecting others doesn't have to include making grand gestures, and it also doesn't have to cost a dime.

Respect is the consideration for others and yourself.

Let's imagine that you are at the bank waiting in line to cash a check. The person ahead of you just finished a long conversation with the teller over a personal financial matter and was shouting and cursing. You walk up to the counter and see that the teller is frustrated and frazzled. You smile and politely greet the teller before asking for the paperwork to cash your check. The distracted teller gives you the incorrect amount of cash, short-changing you by $100. Instead of rudely yelling, you merely show the teller how much cash you received and ask for the additional money.

In this example, you displayed respect by both greeting the bank teller before asking for the paperwork to cash your check and politely requesting the proper amount of money. Instead of rushing the bank teller or getting frustrated with them for giving you the incorrect amount of cash, you remained respectful. Respecting others when they make a mistake or need encouragement lends itself to also respecting yourself.

Respecting yourself allows you to live with dignity. Self-respect includes taking care of yourself properly and the manner in which you present yourself. Every woman has individual needs in order to feel healthy and radiant; for example, how frequently you eat in a day and how long you sleep. If you need seven hours of sleep every night to feel energized, respect yourself by making a good night's sleep a priority to make sure you get those seven hours. Respecting yourself will make you look and feel better, too. You're more likely to be happy and live a fulfilled, thriving life when you respect yourself.

Another way to respect is yourself is based on how you present yourself. What you wear each day displays your level of self-respect. Instead of carelessly wearing clothing that isn't appropriate for the occasion or is revealing and too tight on your body, you can be intentional with your appearance to present yourself respectfully. When meeting friends for afternoon tea at The Blue Box Café, instead of wearing a bodycon dress with a plunging neckline paired with stinky, old sneakers, you would wear a blouse that adequately covers your bosom and coordinates stylishly with trousers or a pleated skirt with stylish pumps.

INTEGRITY

Integrity is your ability to be honest and truthful. When you are honest about your feelings and opinions, you can have more productive, fruitful conversations and relationships. People cherish the truth over false statements. Telling someone what you think they want to hear in an attempt of getting on their 'good side' is not how to live with integrity. Instead, being honest and sharing your truth in a kind and tactful manner is how you would apply integrity properly.

Integrity plays a significant role in everyday life. What do you do when you think no one is watching? What do you say about people when they aren't in your company? A woman with integrity values honesty and always strives to be truthful.

Living with integrity is a matter of consistently being truthful and living in alignment with who you want to be. When you don't live with integrity, you can have a physical response to alert you when you lack it.

For example, upon ordering one David Yurman Cable Classics bracelet with diamonds, you receive two in the mail. You take the box, receipt, and the two bracelets and drive to your local David Yurman store, to return the second bracelet. In this situation, you had the integrity to return the extra bracelet, instead of keeping an item you didn't order or pay for. No one may have known or noticed that you received a second bracelet for free, but living honestly requires you to live by truth instead of deceit or deception.

Living with integrity plays a large role in everyday life because at home, at work, and with family or friends, you have to be accountable to yourself without someone always peering over your shoulder. Integrity empowers you to do what is right, not what is convenient or easy.

> *Integrity is doing what is right, not what is easy.*

Integrity requires a daily commitment to living a virtuous life. Every situation can be handled with integrity; it's a matter of making the right choice, although it can be challenging. And it can be very hard to choose to do what is indeed the right thing to do, not what you may *want* to do.

Integrity is often a nice concept to ponder, but in some cases, it is difficult to live by. In Chapter 1, Mastering Your Mindset, we reviewed the concept of your inner critic and two consciences. Your consciences are a beautiful thing, and your positive conscience will gently guide and remind you how to apply integrity in your life. Whether or not you listen to your positive conscience, it will always prompt you to navigate situations with integrity. You have the option to listen to it and comply or completely ignore it.

When you're out of integrity, you're not living in accordance with the woman you want to be. Consider your intentions to think about what you say and do before taking action to ensure you are fully displaying who you want to be. For example, you can feel disappointed by heavy rain all weekend when you were hoping for sunshine on Sunday afternoon, so you could have a picnic date in Central Park with your husband after church. If you define yourself as an optimistic and pleasant woman, spending the entire week complaining about the rain on Sunday is living without integrity. Instead, whenever a situation doesn't have the outcome you hoped for, you can ask yourself the Elegant Mindset Question: "What is the good in this situation?" to find the silver lining.

When you lack integrity by lying, being deceitful, or living out of alignment with who you want to be, you may, at times, notice a physical response that catches your attention. Knots could form in your stomach, muscles could clench in your throat, or a sense of regret could wash over you. This is your body and mind telling you that you're missing integrity.

Integrity is about being aware of what the honest choice is in a situation, as well as making the conscious decision to select the honest option. This applies in your actions and lifestyle, in both personal and professional situations, whether someone is by your side watching your every move or you're alone and on your own.

HONOR

Honor refers to fairness, being just, and abiding by rules and standards that are established. When something is fair, it is unbiased. Generally speaking, laws and rules aim to be fair and just, providing guiding principles for actions that are acceptable and not acceptable in society. As an honorable woman, you have the moral strength to evaluate a situation and decipher when some laws or rules are unjust and happen to be biased.

Carrying yourself with grace lends itself to leading an honorable life. In every situation, doing what is fair requires you to follow logic and facts instead of prejudice and opinions. Maintaining your sense of honor means you are consistently living justly, and you never waver, even when doing so comes at the expense of comfort or convenience.

For example, as an elementary school teacher, you may have a few students that you strongly connect with and are your 'favorites' in class, but only selecting those few students to speak during a discussion or receive extra credit is a dishonorable way to lead a classroom. Being honorable as a teacher requires you to give all your students equal, fair treatment, even the obnoxious and disruptive ones.

When you live with honor, you gracefully treat others with fairness and equality. At times, what is honorable is not what is according to law or rules, but your positive conscience knows the difference between fair, equal treatment of others, and biased, prejudiced treatment. As with integrity, your positive conscience will gently guide and remind you how to apply honor to a situation and notify you when you miss the mark.

Honor applies fairness and equality to every person and circumstance.

Honor, like integrity, is easy to exemplify in situations when it works to your favor and is the comfortable and convenient option for you to choose. But the truth of the matter is that living honorably means you are consistent in your choices to be fair and just at *all* times.

COMPASSION

Compassion refers to the awareness of understanding and ability to share concern and sensitivity for others. Also known as empathy, compassion is always appreciated and highly valued. When you display concern and care for someone suffering or facing a misfortunate circumstance, you are exercising compassion.

Compassion is the consideration always to think, "People first." Customer service operators on a 1-800 phone line think, "People first." Your junior staff that reports to you at work think, "People first." The wait staff at your local country club think, "People first." Regardless of who you encounter, where they are from, or what they do for a living, all people are first and foremost *people* with thoughts and feelings.

When you treat someone as a store clerk, employee, or waiter without giving them the kindness and concern they deserve, you lack compassion.

On an iconic visit to New York City from London in 1989, Princess Diana displayed compassion beautifully when she picked up and hugged a seven-year-old boy with AIDS. This was at the height of the disease's epidemic, and she shocked the world by doing this kind act with no protective gear. In her life, she modeled and embodied the true meaning of compassion.

In your life, you may or may not truly know the troubles others may experience or endure in their personal or professional lives, which is why compassion is so important. When you have compassion for people around you, you will sympathize with and support them during difficult times. During tragedy, friends and family will appreciate receiving compassion from you as they grieve and recover. You can be compassionate in a variety of ways, from embracing someone with a hug to sharing a kind, encouraging word to providing assistance during a hard time.

Your ability to show kindness to others during difficulty is a measure of your ability to give grace to people during a time of need. Everyone deserves grace, which is the kindness and generosity to emotionally, mentally, and spiritually have support through conflict and adversity. When you give grace to others by showing compassion, you also pay it forward for yourself to receive compassion when you need it most.

Compassion is giving kind concern to others during times of difficulty.

For example, when walking around downtown, you can show compassion to people begging for money by giving them cash or the change clinking in the bottom of your handbag instead of ignoring them as you pass by.

Kindness is cherished most when it's unexpected. Showing compassion requires you to go the extra mile by doing something from the goodness of your heart. Because people don't ever expect compassion, you are giving them a beautiful gift that brightens their day during a difficult time. I often wonder what type of world we would live in if everyone gave compassion freely to one another, without expecting anything in return.

DEPENDABILITY

Dependability refers to the ability to fulfill all the commitments you make. Being dependable is displayed through your actions. If you are trustworthy and reliable, people know they can rely upon you to do what you commit to doing. The practice of dependability can either open new doors or close off opportunities for you. People enjoy being around others that they know they can count on instead of people that are fickle and flaky.

Dependability comes into play in both big and small ways. For example, say you serve on the events committee of your local Junior League chapter, and you agree to turn in a report by 9 AM Tuesday morning with cost estimates from nine venue options for your annual casino fundraising party. If you are dependable, then you will fulfill the commitment and share your research findings with committee members on Tuesday morning, if not earlier. If you are not dependable, you will share the report whenever you make it a priority and decide to complete it, perhaps Wednesday at 12 PM, or Friday at 4 PM.

Dependability empowers your word to be your bond. It is what you do, not what you say. If you make a commitment and don't deliver, you let yourself and others down, showing you can't be trusted and shouldn't be taken seriously. Every commitment, big or small, is important. After promising or committing to something, being dependable means that you will get it done. There are no excuses or exceptions once you make a commitment.

> *Dependability is the ability to follow through on commitments.*

Consider this, if you tell your niece you will take her to the movies on Friday evening, being at her home, on time, to pick her up for the movies is a display of dependability. If an injury, accident, or emergency occurs, your niece will understand the need to reschedule; but in the event that you fail to pick her up because you didn't add it to your calendar or decided to get a manicure instead, you are displaying an unreliable nature.

Repeatedly making commitments and not fulfilling them leads to disappointing others and does not display dependability. What you do when you make a commitment shows people whether you are dependable or not.

COURAGE

Courage refers to the ability to find strength and overcome something that is difficult or frightening. In most cases, you must be exercising courage any time you have integrity, are respectful, or are honorable. It can be difficult to live a life with integrity, respect, and honor because, as previously mentioned, the importance is on doing what is right, not what is comfortable or convenient. Courage is the inner strength that helps you to perform challenging tasks, what you may at times think are impossible tasks, to achieve ultimate greatness.

When you have courage, you recognize discomfort or fear, but you rise above the challenge to be successful. Being unsure of something doesn't stop you or hold you back from pursuing it when you have courage.

Living an elegant life takes courage. For example, upon arriving at your resort for a weeklong vacation, you venture to the hotel to check in and freshen up before enjoying lunch by the pool. As you walk up to the counter, you're greeted by a scowling face, rude tone of voice, and snappy attitude. The receptionist seems to be having a bad day, and she is taking it out on you, unfortunately. You communicate your gracious demeanor with a calm voice, gentle smile, and proper posture, thanks to applying courage.

It takes courage to be honest. It takes courage to treat people pleasantly with kindness after being disrespected. It takes courage to abide by rules and treat people fairly. Courage doesn't make things easy — courage makes them possible. Telling a tiny 'white lie' is easy. Paying an insult with an insult is easy. Breaking the rules when you think no one will find out or notice is easy. Courage makes living your life with a Decorum Code possible because every principle that you regard as important relies on courage to apply it in your life.

Courage doesn't make living morally easy— courage makes it possible.

In Chapter 2, Graceful Self-Discovery, we explored the empowering journey of becoming familiar with who you truly are. It takes courage to embrace yourself sincerely and share who you are with others. Having courage is not an easy thing to do. Courage is one of the values that may require development. Building up your courage is easily done by overcoming a small fear or challenge, then continuing to use courage for more substantial obstacles that may come your way. As you continue to rely on courage, the ability to use it as an anchor for your strength becomes easier over time.

PERSEVERANCE

Perseverance refers to your unwavering ability to overcome difficulties and achieve success, the accomplishment of an objective or purpose. The way you define success is ultimately up to you. Success isn't about having a closet full of Chanel bags or driving a BMW convertible, but it is about you setting a goal or objective for yourself and being able to achieve it. Perseverance kicks in when you have to push through a challenge in order to reach your success.

While working full-time and managing a household of four (yourself, your husband, and your two children) it takes courage for you to pursue a Ph.D. degree in your career field. It will not be easy. But with perseverance, you can accomplish it, and once you have your doctorate, you will undoubtedly be happy that you did. Perseverance is the powerful force that gives you strength to push past difficulty to fulfill your dreams.

Perseverance is the best companion for you on the road to success.

You will face challenges on the path toward achieving your goals. As such, know you are not alone. Few people achieve all of their goals overnight and with little effort. Perseverance is the secret to success because it blesses you with motivation, inspiration, and energy to diligently commit to your achievement. It would be rare for you to build a billion-dollar empire or win a political election while kicking your heels up every day and relaxing on a chaise lounge with a glass of Merlot. You'll have to work for your success – both personally and professionally – and you'll have to work hard. Perseverance helps us to do many things we dream about but assume are out of reach. Becoming fluent in a new language, switching careers fields, and starting a business all require perseverance.

Starting any new endeavor takes perseverance. There may be days when you may feel like giving up on achieving your goals, as if it's useless to bother even pursuing them. Those are the days when perseverance matters the most. Despite obstacles in your way that seem to prevent you from achieving your goals, perseverance will give you the tenacity to follow through and never give up. Unwavering determination means that nothing will stop you from achieving your goals. If you have your heart set on doing something, the only thing in the world that can prevent you from achieving it is you. You decide whether you accomplish your goals or not. It may not be an easy task, but it is possible with perseverance. You have the choice of what your future becomes, based on what you do today.

LOYALTY

Loyalty refers to giving constant and unwavering support or allegiance to a person or organization. Loyalty is expressed whether the recipient is aware of the allegiance or not. In most social relationships, there is an assumption that people are loyal. Friends, colleagues, and acquaintances assume that everyone is loyal to one another; however, true loyalty is hard to find.

Encouraging and supporting your friends and family instead of gossiping or chastising them is a display of loyalty. For example, if your friend recently learned she is pregnant, and you share how horrible of a mother she will be to your aunt over afternoon tea, that is disloyalty, not loyalty.

When you are not supportive of family, friends, colleagues, and co-workers, you are not loyal. Loyalty requires you to maintain your commitment to loved ones at all times, having their best interest at heart.

You may not always agree with the things people say and do, but when you are loyal, you spend more time accepting their actions and supporting them rather than criticizing or gossiping about them.

Loyalty and respect go hand in hand.

When you are loyal to someone, you respect them. Being considerate of others includes non-judgmental help and encouragement. When you are loyal, you hold yourself to a higher standard. True friends are loyal friends. They continue to encourage and stay present in the lives of people they care about, even when situations are difficult or challenging. Loyalty is invaluable and an extraordinary bond, shared between people that care, comfort, cheer, and celebrate with others through the ups and downs in life.

REPUTATION MANAGEMENT

Your character, the values that you believe in and live by, shape your reputation. This is the influence and true power of core values. A person can say anything under the sun, claiming to be respectful or loyal, but your actions display to others who you truly are. It's easy to say you are elegant, dependable, and compassionate, but the choices you make on a daily basis ultimately define you.

What you do on a regular basis defines your character.

Your reputation is not only essential but influential. The reputation you have precedes you. Upon mentioning your name in a conversation, someone has a thought or idea about who you are if they have met you or crossed paths with you before. Your reputation motivates how others think and feel about you. If someone wants to date you, hire you, or invite you to join an organization, your reputation plays a role in whether or not they actually will. Opportunities for you are either opened or closed because of your reputation. How you treat others says a lot about you and your character. Your future truly lies in the hands of your reputation.

When you live with je ne sais quoi, according to your Decorum Code, you are proactively managing your reputation. You are deciding who you want to be and how you want others to perceive you, then living your life to be in alignment with those values so you can control your reputation. As we explored in Chapter 2, Graceful Self-Discovery, it's vitally important (after deciding who you want to be) that you live your life in a manner that supports it. When you align your actions with your values, you live a congruent lifestyle.

On the contrary, when your actions and values are not aligned, you live an incongruent lifestyle. Your personal light shines the brightest when living out your truth and being the woman that you want to be. The best part about your Decorum Code is that it is entirely within your control. You decide what values are important and how to best live those values out in your life.

Actionable Advice

You can create the reputation that you want to have by cultivating the values you want to be known for.

Take a moment and write in your journal how you want to be described when you aren't in the room. What do you want to be known for? What values? How will you treat people? How will you handle and manage stressful situations? Describe yourself in a paragraph or two.

After writing the statement of how you want to be perceived and known by others, make a list of supportive actions you need to take in order to embody those values.

For example, if you wrote that you want to be on time for all appointments and meetings, think about what you can do to make that happen. The supportive action for being polished and punctual is to manage your time so you can plan ahead for how long it will take to get dressed, travel to the appointment, and find the exact location all while arriving 10 minutes early instead of 10 minutes late.

* * * * *

CREATING YOUR DECORUM CODE

Your Decorum Code can include as many values as you desire. My recommendation is to include a minimum of three character values. Three values will serve as a solid foundational set for your personal core values in this empowering statement. Your Decorum Code includes your core values and your chic credo. It's a statement that serves as a guide for creating the best life you can have because it will inspire you to be the best woman you can be.

With your Decorum Code, you define the woman you want to be.

Actionable Advice

The first sentence of your Decorum Code includes your name and the one word that you selected from Chapter 2, Graceful Self-Discovery, to describe yourself.

Include at least three core values in your Core Value Set. You are free to select as many core values as you desire, carefully choosing the values that you want to be known for and that you intend to carry out in your daily life.

Choosing a value that is not something you will strive to live by is a missed opportunity to get the full power from your Decorum Code. Instead, select core values for yourself that are already in alignment with the lifestyle that you currently live or part of the lifestyle that you want to live. Be authentic and select core values that represent who you truly are and how you want to be perceived.

Once you confirm your core values, it's time to write down your Decorum Code!

The script I suggest for your Decorum Code includes the following:

I am _____ [Your first and last name] a _____ [your descriptive word from Chapter 2, Graceful Self-Discovery] woman.

A woman of _____, _____, and _____ [List all of your core values].

I choose to live every day standing firmly in my power as a lady.

I am confident, graceful, beautiful, intelligent, and capable of anything I put my mind to.

I abide by these values as a commitment to be the best woman that I can truly be—me: _____ [Your first and last name].

*****

USING YOUR DECORUM CODE

After writing your Decorum Code in your journal, write it again on a separate piece of paper and keep it conveniently tucked in an easy-to-access location, like your top bedside table drawer.

Now, you have this empowering personal statement to refer to as often as you wish. A regular review of your Decorum Code, including daily readings aloud every morning or evening, will inspire and remind you of the woman you need to be every day. Your Decorum Code provides counsel for addressing every possible interaction or encounter you may come across. A powerful reference tool, your Decorum Code prompts you to be the woman you want to be and helps you harmoniously align your values with your actions.

THE DECORUM CODE ANNUAL REVIEW

At the beginning of each new year, you can review your Decorum Code to determine if it still aligns with who you are and who you want to be. As women, we evolve over time. We grow. We learn. We refine. Our perspective on life changes as we change. Your Decorum Code should always accurately reflect you and your core values in the current moment. As such, an annual assessment of your Decorum Code is vital to maintaining its significance and truth.

Elegantly living with je ne sais quoi is best achieved with guidance, which is why I created the Decorum Code to be a constant reminder for what to say, do, and think in situations when you may feel caught off guard or put on the spot. Daily readings of your Decorum Code lay the foundation on which you will rely when you encounter challenges or find yourself in a pinch.

OWNING YOUR PERSONAL POWER

Everything you say and do shows others what values you hold, which directly influence your reputation. It's best to actively create your reputation around your values than to allow other people to define you for themselves. There is confidence in defining who you want to be and owning your personal power. A life with elegance is a life lead by confidence. Once you embrace your Decorum Code, you will start to feel more radiant and remarkable. That is no coincidence. An elegant life is a confident life.

Chic Character Secrets

- Your character governs what you think, say, and do, based on your beliefs.

- To be elegant and empowered, decide who you want to be and live your life according to those principles.

- Write your Decorum Code in both your journal and on a separate piece of paper, keeping the document stashed in a location that is easy to access.

- Read your Decorum Code daily to refresh and remind yourself how to live gracefully in all encounters, both good and bad.

CHAPTER 8

POLISHED PRESENCE

Charm them with your presence as soon as they look at you.

Anna Held

A life with je ne sais quoi is undoubtedly charming. Your sense of charm is expressed and displayed through your presence. Whether it's the twinkle in your eye as you enjoy a casual conversation with a friend over a cup of afternoon tea, or it's your dazzling smile as you listen to your husband tell you about his wonderful day at the dinner table, your charming presence is always a constant in a life with je ne sais quoi.

Your presence, also known as your aura, is the energy that you create and give to others when they are around you. Your presence easily displays your mood and thoughts. In Chapter 12, Captivating Communication, we will explore the topic of body language, which plays a large role in your presence as well. But for now, we will focus on the intangible quality of an elegant presence: the captivating, compelling fundamental quality known as charm.

Charm, known as having a charismatic presence, is the genuine ability to connect with people and inspire their enthusiasm, interest, or approval. At its core, charm is a combination of social and emotional skills put to work, eliciting favorable feelings from others around you. Charm is a graceful superpower, helpful for navigating personal and professional relationships with delight. Interacting with acquaintances, friends, family, and coworkers using charm puts them at ease around you. Charm is an elegant character trait that enhances both your life and the lives of others around you.

An elegant woman is easily recognized by the charming manner in which she carries herself.

Although charm is immeasurable, it can be easily identified and is always appreciated. When you are charming, you express your emotions and communicate with others in an authentic, sensitive, and graceful manner. In displaying your charm, you easily motivate and inspire the best qualities in others, making them a joy to be around, work for, and work with. The ability you have to make others feel important and recognized is an elegant, timeless quality in your personality.

A warm, inviting way to display your charm every day is with an authentic smile. When you smile, you connect with someone in a welcoming, delightful manner. Smiling makes others feel pleasant, and according to widely known scientific studies, smiling can improve your feelings with a sprinkling of pleasantness, too!

When it comes to charm, some people are born with it while others have to develop it. There's a common misconception that if you don't have the 'it factor' (charm), then you never will.

I want to let you in on a secret: charm is a skill that can be developed and refined. Every woman has the ability to be captivating and compelling, alluring others with charm.

In order to be charming, there are four areas to master: confidence, pleasantness, mindfulness, and intentionality. The recipe for charm is the combination of all these elements together, instead of lacking one or two.

CHARM WITH CONFIDENCE

When you are confident, you live your best life. By being firmly certain in who you are and your abilities, you can appreciate the pleasant qualities about yourself and be open to finding pleasant qualities in others. Confidence helps you to feel your best and share the best version of yourself with the world.

Everyone on this planet is blessed with gifts and talents. Being confident allows you to comfortably stand straight and walk tall with assurance, not arrogance. When you are charming and confident, you know that it's best to complement others, not compete with them. Your charming nature allows you to have an open mind when interacting with others to determine if or how you can help them accomplish or achieve something.

For example, say you volunteer with your child's parent-teacher association. At an upcoming fundraiser, you are asked to give a speech. Confidence empowers you to prepare your notes, rehearse, and proudly take the stage. Your belief in what you will share during your presentation can motivate and inspire you to give your best effort with charm during your moment to shine in the spotlight.

CHARM WITH PLEASANTNESS

When you are pleasant, you share joy with others. Pleasantness is your ability to maintain and spread optimism with others. Being charming is about inspiring positivity in others, and the only way to do that effectively is to be positive yourself.

You can always choose to be pleasant in any situation. It's all about perspective. Even when you are having a bad day, you can choose not to broadcast negativity. Being charming allows you to focus on the positive elements to spend your time and attention on optimism rather than pessimism.

For example, if you are entering the grocery store and see a store clerk standing near the door arranging the front display, you can smile as you pass by them, say hello to greet them, and ask how their day is going. Every interaction with someone is an opportunity for you to share pleasantness, adding a sprinkle of kindness to their day.

CHARM WITH MINDFULNESS

When you are mindful, you are fully present in the moment. Mindfulness is your ability to focus on the conversation or situation at hand and give it your full attention. Practicing mindfulness allows you to truly connect with others and be completely engaged in everything you do.

When speaking with someone, instead of anxiously fidgeting or routinely checking your watch every few minutes, you can be mindful by focusing on the moment, standing or sitting still, and paying attention to the words being said. Dismiss all distractions and shut off electronic devices to be fully engaged during discussions. The words exchanged should have enough passion and power to hold your interest.

Everyone is fascinating. Each person has a unique story, incredible talents, interesting goals, and amazing accomplishments. You merely need to get to know someone to find out their fascinating factor. Taking a genuine interest in others is about enjoying each and every conversation, instead of hearing what someone says but not really listening to them.

Hearing is the physical activity of words and sounds hitting your ears. Listening requires that you hear the words people say to you and process the information being shared. When you are genuinely interested in others, you are fully engaged by attentively making eye contact and leaning your body forward slightly to maintain your focus.

For example, when standing in line for a morning shot of espresso, listening requires you to pay attention to the woman in front of you as she excitedly shares a story about her son winning a soccer tournament instead of contemplating which bouquet of flowers — roses or tulips — to pick up from the farmer's market that afternoon. Mindfulness allows you to be an active participant in every conversation, listening for both context and clarity.

CHARM WITH INTENTIONALITY

Intentionality is one of the main elements of living elegantly and also plays a big role in being charming. When you are thoughtful with your actions, you can apply intention to lead with charm, being confident, pleasant, and mindful in what you say and do.

Being intentional allows you to carefully select your words, actions, and body language in every situation instead of doing what is convenient or relying on your initial reaction. Intention is the powerful guidance that inspires you to think courtesy first, which helps you to display yourself with a warm, inviting, charming presence.

For example, when picking up three dress suits from the dry cleaners, and the garments are not clean and ready at their scheduled time, you can be intentional by maintaining your composure as you speak to the manager about needing your clothing for an upcoming trip you have tomorrow. Intentionality allows you to select composure instead of recklessly cursing or yelling over the counter about your dry cleaning not being prepared at its promised time.

LIVING WITH A CHARMING PRESENCE

Living with charm is more about courtesy than comfort. When you are charming, you are delightful to be around, and you inspire delight in others. Creating a life with charm allows you to dazzle the people around you with your captivating presence. Once you live with charm, you will find that life is more enjoyable and fulfilling. Having a polished presence differs from simply looking elegant and sophisticated. You can easily be stylish but not charming. If you lack the social skills necessary to interact with people in a delightful manner, your presence is the missing link to achieving your full elegance.

TRANSFORMING YOUR CHARMING PRESENCE

Daily practice of the four characteristics of charm will transform your presence. Small gestures have a grand impact. You can add a touch of confidence to your demeanor, be pleasant with others, gracefully be mindful during conversations, and apply intention to everything you do.

Whether you are speaking with a librarian to find your favorite book, or on a two-hour-long phone conversation with your best friend, you can consistently be a joy to be around, no matter how long or short the encounter may be.

Unless you are intentional, you will likely showcase how you feel in your interactions with others when you are feeling tired, stressed, or irritable. Living with je ne sais quoi requires you to consciously decide how you will act and what you will say, even at times when you may not feel like being delightful.

To transform your polished presence, I recommend mastering one area of charm at a time then adding another to be fully empowered and elegant.

MASTERING YOUR CHARMING PRESENCE WITH CONFIDENCE

If you lack confidence and tend to carry yourself with uncertainty, shame, or doubt, you can turn that around by building a strong belief in yourself. When you don't feel comfortable in your own skin, are apologetic about your actions, or use explanations and excuses to justify what you do, those are signs that you may lack confidence.

Because confidence is about knowing who you are and embracing it, self-discovery and self-love are essential. When you don't know yourself, you can't appreciate yourself, which means you can't love yourself and cultivate confidence. Self-awareness is important in helping you recognize the areas where you lack confidence, so you can improve them. You must embrace who you are and offer it to the world, loving yourself fully, with all your talents, skills, and flaws.

Instead of comparing yourself to others, spend time getting to know and love you, the real you. Fill your days with positive affirmations and celebrate every success and accomplishment you achieve.

MASTERING YOUR CHARMING PRESENCE WITH PLEASANTNESS

If you constantly complain, gossip, or find fault with others, you may lack a continuous sense of pleasantness. Being a 'Debbie Downer' may not be a nickname you enjoy, but if others have referred to you with that nickname, you may want to enhance your level of positivity and optimism.

To cultivate more pleasantness in your life, you can focus on gratitude. Being thankful every day for your home, children, income, health, and skillset pulls your attention toward good things instead of negativity. The thoughts you continuously focus on and listen to will drive what you say and do. Be careful to only listen to your positive conscience to create the habit of living with a pleasant, polished mindset.

MASTERING YOUR CHARMING PRESENCE WITH MINDFULNESS

During a conversation, if you are not paying attention to someone and frequently ask them to repeat themselves, you may not be cultivating mindfulness at that moment. A wandering mind is normal; you just have to elegantly guide where it should go, focusing it on the person or task at hand.

To master your mindfulness, remind yourself to actively listen during all conversations. Commit to connecting with every person you encounter and be in the moment. During a conversation, strive to have a meaningful dialogue or interaction. The key is to make the exchange less about you and more about the other person and their needs, experiences, or opinions.

This is not about being submissive or passive in conversation; it's about being compassionate and empathetic, which allows others to feel important and recognized. Mindfulness makes a person feel valued while having a conversation with you.

MASTERING YOUR CHARMING PRESENCE WITH INTENTIONALITY

If you tend to say or do things rashly without carefully thinking about them first, intentionality may be an area of opportunity for you to refine. Being elegant is about giving thought and care to always thinking through everything you say and do to live gracefully.

Take an audit of your words and actions, considering whether or not you were thinking before you spoke or did anything. If you find yourself reflecting on your day and regretting what you said or did, you can start to wake up your mind to think first before doing.

In a conversation, stop to think before you speak. Pausing to take a deep breath and collecting your thoughts before you open your mouth will help you to find the elegant inspiration to speak with eloquence and carry yourself with charm.

Actionable Advice

If you don't feel charming and elegant every day, what area can you improve to enhance your polished presence?

Identify one area of charm you can start to master and write in your journal what daily actions you can take to start being more charming in your interactions. What you think, say, and do repeatedly creates your habits and, as such, matter a great deal regarding your charming presence.

As a delicate reminder, routinely review in your journal the set of daily actions you can practice to master your charming presence.

* * * * *

Your presence displays the manner in which you carry yourself. Being a delightful woman allows you to captivate others with your charm. When you are confident, pleasant, mindful, and intentional, you can gracefully and easily navigate life with charm. Your charming presence can be applied to all encounters, regardless of how long you spend interacting with someone. Charm is a beautiful, lasting impression you can leave lingering in the air upon departing from others, like the intoxicating scent of Diorissimo perfume.

Chic Presence Secrets

- Allow your conversation partner to speak more in a conversation to display your charming presence.

- Smile, make eye contact, and sit or stand straight to convey your interest and attention in every encounter.

- You can be polished and polite in both two-second and two-hour exchanges with someone. The length of time isn't important, but your consistent charming nature is.

- Addressing people by their name is a chic secret to captivating others with your charm.

- Always remember to be confident, pleasant, mindful, and intentional in your actions – and your charm will shine brightly through.

CHAPTER 9

SOCIAL GRACES

*Be pretty if you can,
be witty if you must,
but be gracious if it kills you.*

Elsie de Wolfe

Social graces, also known as elegant actions, are based on the simple principle of respect, which is treating all people with consideration and care. Social graces are contemplated and calculated before being carried out instead of being random thoughts or deeds. Being intentional also impacts your actions, similar to its effect on your presence. In an elegant life with je ne sais quoi, social graces are displayed at all times—consistently, not sporadically, or at the times when you *feel* like it.

Social graces are an essential part of an elegant lifestyle.

A life of elegance strives to make every thought, action, and interaction pleasant and delightful. Instead of being hasty or careless, you carefully make every person you encounter feel warmly welcomed when they interact with you, from speaking with a hostess as you enter a restaurant to chatting with your neighbors at a homeowners association meeting.

Social graces are not just for you; they are for everyone around you as well. Your family, friends, colleagues, and acquaintances benefit from having a positive encounter with you because the sprinkle of positivity you share with them is sure to be carried throughout the rest of their day.

Your character forms the basis for every action you take because what you think, say, and do are based on your distinctive mental and moral qualities. Unfortunately, many people don't take the time to define their character, and they let their feelings drive the decisions when caught in difficult situations, which in turn allows their emotions to determine their character. After exploring character and moral values earlier in this book, in Chapter 7, Compelling Character, you know that what you believe and how you define yourself directly impact how you live.

By now on your journey of creating a life with je ne sais quoi, you probably realize that your repeated actions create your reputation. Your reputation is important because the opinions that people have about you influence how they choose to interact with you, or if they want to at all. Reputations are commonly discussed amongst mixed company. People love to talk, and your reputation is likely a conversation topic when you are not around. Being socially graceful allows your reputation to remain constantly elegant.

THE ESSENCE OF SOCIAL GRACES

The objective of a socially graceful interaction is to always leave people better than you found them. During a brief or lengthy encounter, you can part ways with people feeling better and more positive than before they crossed paths with you. This is the essence of artfully living with social graces.

Being socially graceful also creates an atmosphere that makes it enjoyable for others to be in your company. Displaying social graces includes treating everyone you meet, from the restaurant manager to the busboy, with positivity and kindness. This straightforward principle makes daily tasks and regular interactions a dash more delightful.

DAILY SOCIAL GRACES

In every interaction throughout your day, you can find a delicate way to display kindness with your polished words and polite actions.

In conversations, be socially graceful by making eye contact, paying attention to stay engaged, listening to comprehend what is said, and responding with intriguing phrases or captivating questions. Take a genuine interest in what people say to you and be a delightful conversation partner in all encounters.

Show gratitude to honor someone for doing something kind for you. Say, "Thank you," when appropriate, and follow up with a handwritten thank you card to show gratitude for gifts, overnight stays, and other kind gestures. When people are exceptionally kind to you, they deserve to be appreciated and acknowledged.

Be punctual for personal and professional engagements. Any time you have a scheduled commitment, respect the time of the people involved enough to manage your calendar and show up on time. From attending hair appointments to dental exams to girls' night dinners to work meetings, everything you commit to doing is important, and your punctuality affects the entire day of other people involved.

Consider those around you when in a conversation with someone or speaking on the phone in public places. Be socially graceful by maintaining your voice volume at a considerable level to avoid disrupting or disturbing others. Long phone conversations are best saved for the comfort of your home instead of public places among mixed company.

Politely display your charming demeanor by greeting people with a smile. A simple smile is an inviting way to warmly welcome or depart from someone and is a universal sign of friendliness. Smiling will positively affect both your mood and the mood of those around you.

JE NE SAIS QUOI

Give a hand to others in need when appropriate. As you exit a building and see someone laden with bags, exercise your social gracefulness by holding open the door for them. Small favors, such as opening doors, picking up items off the floor, holding the elevator door, and paying someone a compliment are beautiful acts of kindness you can perform daily.

Whether you are in a casual or fine dining setting, enjoy your meal with a quiet, polite manner. Loudly smacking or slurping is not elegant and should be avoided. Social gracefulness extends throughout your day, even when eating. Maintain your elegance at the table by requesting that someone pass you a food item and chewing with your mouth closed.

Upon enjoying the company of a group of mutual friends or new colleagues, introduce the people that don't know one another. Your ability to foster meaningful connections among a group will be greatly appreciated in both social and work settings. If two people have something in common, such a hobby or hometown, you can introduce them by mentioning the shared interest or background, sparkling the introduction with elegance.

When styled from head to toe, if you wear a hat, be thoughtful and remove it indoors. In venues including the movie theater, symphony, and opera, your hat may block the clear view of those behind you. The courtesy of removing your hat will be appreciated so they can enjoy the show or performance as much as you do.

Avoid scandalous behavior, such as getting drunk at a bar, fist fighting, or loudly arguing in public. Having a good time at a party doesn't have to include you doing something you will be embarrassed about and later regret. When you know your drinking limits, you can enjoy alcoholic beverages in moderation and delightfully respect others around you.

Honor good service at restaurants, salons, and hotels with a thoughtful tip. Waiters, hair stylists, and bellhops who give you exceptional service earned a compliment, a tip, and a smile. Tipping is the most tangible way to show gratitude to those that provide you with a service.

Expand your mind by learning or enhancing yourself with skills. Take classes to learn how to cook, sew, speak a foreign language, or how to improve in any area that interests you to gracefully increase your self-confidence and improve the quality of your life.

JE NE SAIS QUOI

As you become proficient in new skills, you can enjoy using them for personal or professional endeavors.

Enjoy the culture life has to offer by visiting museums, watching dance performances, and attending musical concerts. If you have yet to see the beauty of ballet on stage or hear the enchantment of a symphony performed live, you can enrich your life with new and cultured pursuits.

Upon being invited to a party, always respond within 24 hours to graciously accept or politely decline. Review your calendar to determine if you have conflicts from previously scheduled engagements before you respond.

Arrive at events held at someone's home with a gift for the host or hostess. A candle, bottle of wine, or bouquet of flowers are beautiful ways to show your gratitude and appreciation for the invitation to enjoy a social event taking place in the home of a family member, friend, or loved one.

Before traveling to a foreign country, review the customs and acceptable practices. The manner in which you nod your head or shake hands will differ in countries around the world. Knowing simple conversational phrases such as *Please, Thank You, Yes, No, Hello,* and *Goodbye* will allow you to travel abroad with confidence and candor.

ARTFUL LIVING

Your ability to act with social graces allows you to live artfully, harnessing your feminine power. Maintaining a consistently sweet and charming demeanor is the true definition of living an elegant life. In small, delicate ways, you can make every encounter you experience delightful and leave behind a memorable impression. Your daily actions, attitude, and demeanor create your reputation and serve to represent the essence of your regal character.

Chic Graceful Secrets

- Aim to share positivity and kindness with others, from paying someone a compliment to doing a small favor to assist, when appropriate.

- Let respect be the cornerstone of every word you say and action you take, giving thoughtful consideration to be consistently polite to others.

- Express your gratitude by saying, "Thank you," and sending a handwritten thank you note to someone upon receiving gifts and attending events held in others' homes.

- Take pleasure in the arts by enjoying live dance performances, visiting museums, and attending musical concerts.

PART 4
COMPETENCE

CHAPTER 10

STANDARD OF EXCELLENCE

Every job is a self-portrait of the person who did it. Autograph your work with excellence.

Vince Lombardi

In anything you do, it is best to strive for excellence. Excellence requires that you give something your best effort, not a half-done or weak effort. Your best. The objective is not to attain perfection but to attain excellence.

Everyone will have a different level of 'best' for their personal work ethic, but the amazing thing is that you have the opportunity to define yours. You have the choice to blaze your own trail. You can choose to bring a standard of excellence to everything you do.

Earlier in this book, we explored self-discovery, the ability to uncover and embrace who you are and what you are capable of. In Chapter 2, Graceful Self-Discovery, you identified your talents and passions, and at least one of those skills is something you excel at, if not in a professional capacity, then at least in a personal one.

Now, we'll explore how you can apply your competency to your talents and passions. Competence, your ability to do something efficiently, refers to the skillset you have to thrive and dominate what you do intellectually. A woman with confidence, class, and charm can only go so far in life without competence.

Actionable Advice

Take a moment and ponder what area or skill you have that you are competent in. Then I want you to ask yourself: "Am I good or am I great at this?"

Can you honestly say that you are currently a master or working toward mastery in this area?

Everyone has room for improvement, so perfection is not the goal here—the goal is the pursuit of improvement.

Make a list in your journal of skills that you are 'good' but not 'great' at.

Choose one skill to commit to achieving a standard of excellence in. This could be something you do personally, for fun, or in a professional capacity.

* * * * *

A life with je ne sais quoi is spectacular, remarkable, and amazing, not boring, mundane, or average. There is no point in performing any task at a level less than excellent. When you put forth your best effort, you apply elegance to your work and projects. Giving 50% of your time, effort, and attention when serving on the board of your local Girls Scouts chapter is far from elegant; it's distasteful. A standard of excellence requires you to push the envelope past average and mediocre and aspire for amazing and magnificent, displaying your character and standing out from the crowd. Average work produces average results, which creates an average life. Amazing work produces amazing results, which creates an amazing life.

When you make a commitment, you commit to doing nothing less than you best. You can apply your elegance to work and tasks by being intentional and thoughtful to do things exceptionally well. You'll have a sense of pride and accomplishment after a job well done, too.

Never give less than your best.

Whatever you do, wherever you do it, always give maximum effort. Instead of earning the reputation of a slacker, you should strive to incorporate a standard of excellence in everything you do. When you contribute to a task or project by giving very little effort, it shows. You know it (even if you may not want to admit it), and everyone around you knows it.

This is commonly reflected in your career but also shows up in your personal life. If you lead a weekly Bible study group in your neighborhood or serve as the mom-in-charge of snacks for your daughter's cheerleading squad, it's best to not only fulfill commitments you make for projects but also to exceed expectations and commitments. Whether you are in a personal or professional environment, anytime you agree to do something, give it every ounce of effort and attention you have.

Your standard of excellence reflects your character.

Doing a decent job is easy. Giving minimal effort is convenient. Doing the bare minimum is comfortable. But the truth is, someone that is passionate about what they're doing would never even consider doing a merely decent job on a task. When you truly enjoy what you do, you want to do your best.

Why else should you do something, other than to do it exceedingly well? Doing your best always pays off. We are all only human; therefore, room for improvement is to be expected. However, focusing your time and attention on doing the best job possible for the task at hand always yields a more successful outcome. When you apply a level of excellence to your task, you improve the work of others by showing up to share your best effort, talents, and energy.

Can you think of someone in your life that dominates what they do? Who thinks outside the box, always brings high energy, and wordlessly communicates their passion for their craft? Most of us have at least one person that fits this profile, either from a past or present experience. Their enthusiasm motivates their standard of excellence, and it probably motivates you, too.

Consider this: what is the motivation behind the level of effort you give?

As an elegant woman, the purpose of completing a task isn't to cross it off your to-do list. The purpose is to do it with your heart and soul. Being intentional with how you spend your time, you should be passionate about what you do. When you're passionate about what you do, you will give nothing less than your best.

Actionable Advice

Think about all the commitments you have in your life, both your personal and professional obligations. This includes your job and any extracurricular organizations you are involved in, as a member or leader.

In your journal, make a list of two columns.

On the left column, write down your role for each task or project you regularly spend time doing.

On the right column, rate yourself on a scale of 1-10, with 1 being the lowest and 10 being the highest, based on the level of effort you currently bring to each role.

Take a moment and rate your work ethic for each role you currently have. Be honest with yourself about your performance and contributions.

As an example, your list may look something like this:

Wife	9
Mother	10
Sales Director	4
Local Red Cross Volunteer	5
Church Membership Committee Volunteer	7
Women's Networking Group Event Coordinator	3
Neighborhood Mother's Group Leader	2

* * * * *

The past can't be changed, but the future holds a new beginning. I encourage you to review your list to look at every role you currently have and ask yourself: "Why is any role lower than a 10?" Why have you given *less* than your best effort in any area of your personal or professional life?

Before making any changes, it's best to identify the reason why you haven't applied your standard of excellence to every role you fulfill. Knowing why you aren't currently giving your best helps you to identify improvements for the future. We all continue to evolve as we experience life. You may have enjoyed a particular role or organization when you were initially hired or committed to a position, but maybe you no longer have the passion that you once did. We change as we grow and develop, and there is no shame in evolving your elegant self! Your work and social commitments should change along with you.

The areas in which you may be giving less excellence could be your job or a volunteer opportunity, and I want you to reflect on what's holding you back from giving your best and exceeding expectations. Why are you just *good* and not *great*? What has kept you from being excellent in all that you do? You may not be passionate about something related to your job role. You may have committed to fulfilling a volunteer position that no longer ignites your passion. Or perhaps you committed to fulfilling a role that you were never passionate about, but you felt obligated to accept for whatever reason.

Today is a new day, and in the spirit of striving for a standard of excellence, it's time to make a change. For all responsibilities in your life that you currently fulfill and are giving less than a 10 in, spend time exploring the motivation behind your lack of commitment and work ethic to each responsibility. And make a change, if necessary.

For example, you may have rated yourself as giving a 4 for effort at work. Perhaps you can explore a new job role if you no longer enjoy the responsibilities in your current job. Or you may have given yourself a 5 for effort for volunteering at a non-profit organization. Perhaps you can explore a different volunteer position at the same organization or a similar volunteer position at a different organization.

THE BENEFITS OF EXCELLENCE

There are several advantages to having a standard of excellence. When you are excited about what you're doing, you bring an innovative perspective to your tasks and projects. A standard of excellence earns respect from others. Praise and pride are the rewards for a job well done.

When you outshine beyond the limits of what you thought you could do, you are able to tap into your true abilities and maximize your full potential.

ACHIEVING YOUR FULL POTENTIAL

Everyone has greatness within them. I believe that most people, regardless of gender, don't maximize their full potential. They complete tasks comfortably and over time may slightly increase their effort, but they rarely strive for greatness.

You don't know the heights of success you can achieve if you've never pursued maximizing your greatness. Women are quick to downplay their talents and treasures, regularly 'playing it safe' and never 'pushing the limits.' If you're headed toward the promotion, award, or degree you truly want, fear can stop you in your tracks, discouraging you from chasing after your dreams with relentless fire and energy to achieve your full potential.

One thing I know for sure is that if you keep doing what you've always done, you will see the results you've always gotten. If you want something different, you have to do something different.

There is more to life than working in a place that makes you unhappy or attending meetings for an organization when you quietly wish you were somewhere else. None of us can have a perfect life, but we can all work toward a life that we'll love.

To start achieving your full potential, you can create a proactive plan to take charge and elevate your life. After discovering your talents and passions, you can strive for mastery in those areas, leverage your God-given abilities, and maximize your greatness.

Giving your best effort to your skills and passions may just surprise you. Achieving your full potential can show you that you're far more talented than you give yourself credit for.

AWAKEN YOUR PERSONAL POWER

Your personal power is your ability to be the best version of yourself, leading with confidence and leveraging your skills. Your personal power is a level of strength that comes from within, and it's the key to an elegant, thriving life with je ne sais quoi. Also known as your zone of genius, your personal power is a balance between being content with your skills and continuously striving for improvement to reach the next level.

Tapping into your personal power is rare and remarkable. When you show up as the best woman: wife, mother, friend, and employee that you can be, you affect massive change. You have the honor of making an impact in this world in a fantastic, awe-inspiring way. Think about how different the world would be if we all lived in the realm of our personal power. We would have better school systems, more profitable companies, healthier communities, and happier homes if we all maximized our true potential and tapped into our personal power.

For example, if you are an avid swimmer and you love to hit the pool, you could become a certified swim instructor and volunteer to teach children living in an orphanage the critical life skill of swimming. You are not only giving your time to others in need, but you're tapping into your passion (and personal power) to teach them a life-saving skill and helping empower them, so they never have to be afraid of going for a swim.

When you don't tap into your personal power, you may feel unfulfilled in life without knowing why.

If it takes significant energy to 'wind yourself up' or force yourself to do an adequate job for a task, you are outside the scope of your personal power. When you are not fulfilled in one area of your life, the negativity may often carry over to other areas of your life.

For example, say you are a creative director at a marketing agency. After nine years at the firm, you no longer get excited about fonts, colors, and logos. If you decide to stay in the job to pay your mortgage and your son's private school tuition, your work performance may fall outside the realm of your personal power. You may start to receive low scores on quarterly performance reviews and lose interest in your favorite pastime: oil painting on canvas. When you notice the chain reaction of how unhappiness from your job negatively affects other areas of your life, you may have the 'wake-up call' you need to start making changes where necessary to get your life back on track.

Strive for all the areas of your life to fully serve you, ensuring that you have a high level of vibrancy or state of being.

Contributing to the world with your personal power will have you feeling invigorated, energized, and inspired to attain more success than you ever dreamed of. I encourage you to create your life by giving nothing less than a standard of excellence to your pursuits.

STRIVING FOR MASTERY

Whatever skill or area of mastery you have, it's important to commit yourself to continuous learning and refinement in order to maintain a standard of excellence. Regardless of your age, you are a student, continuously learning about the world around you. Embrace your intellectual curiosity and apply it to your skillset, too.

Make ongoing learning a part of your lifestyle to continue to be highly competent in your skills and talents. Some professional fields, such as the legal industry, require ongoing learning to maintain your state or national license. Other professional fields, such as the information technology industry, regularly require certifications due to their fast-paced and increasingly changing nature. Whether your job requires ongoing education or not, you can set the criteria for yourself to commit to a particular number of hours or resources every week, month, or year to keep your skills sharp.

One good recommendation for continuing to learn is reading at least one book every month related to your job function, skillset, or industry. Reading or listening to books gives you a fresh perspective and can spark creative ideas for your work or projects. In addition to reading books, you can explore other avenues to expand your knowledge, including conferences, workshops, certifications, webinars, and podcasts.

YOUR STANDARD OF EXCELLENCE

Defining a standard of excellence for yourself is an empowering advantage you will have in your personal and professional life. Once you define exactly what your standards entail when you make decisions or take actions, you can keep yourself accountable by verifying that what you do is aligned with your standards.

For example, if one of your standards is to be on time for meetings and engagements regularly, then that standard requires you to plan your day in advance to ensure that you can meet it. If you know that it will cause you to be late, you are less likely to run to the nail salon for a last-minute pedicure right before meeting friends for cocktails. That would violate your personal standards of excellence. So instead, you schedule your nail appointment at a different time, so you can be prompt for your social session over martinis.

Actionable Advice

Are you ready to elevate your life by creating your personal standards?

In your journal, write your Personal Standards of Excellence, including a requirement for yourself regarding every responsibility you have and any general guidelines you want to include for your life. These principles will dictate your personal level of giving your best to everything that you do. Your Personal Standards of Excellence will become your daily objectives for how you fulfill all the responsibilities in your life.

For example, your Personal Standards of Excellence may look something like this:

<u>My Personal Standards of Excellence</u>

Wife: I will be kind to and patient with my husband, always listening to hear his point of view and being open to trying his ideas.

Mother: I will continue to make my children the priority in my life and do my best to attend 75% of their activities and performances. I will tuck them into bed every night.

Sales Director: I will arrive at work promptly on time every day. I will take only positive energy to the office in order to motivate my team. I will be engaged in our division's goals and projects to drive revenue for the company continuously. I will hire a leadership training coach to learn how to be a more effective leader and meet them once a month for continuous learning and refinement.

Local Red Cross Volunteer: I will attend all meetings for my committee and be an active participant.

Church Membership Committee Volunteer: I will be five minutes early for my once-a-month volunteer shifts at church. I will brainstorm and bring one new idea to discuss at each quarterly committee meeting.

~~Women's Networking Group Event Coordinator:~~ I will resign from this position and use this as a learning opportunity to always step down from commitments I am not passionate about.

~~Neighborhood Mother's Group Leader:~~ I will continue to be a member and transition leadership responsibilities to my neighbor, Genevieve.

As a woman, I will carry myself with integrity and dependability every day and be honest and reliable at all times. I will be on time for every appointment, engagement, and commitment. I will give every responsibility I have committed to my best effort so that I can be proud of my work and volunteerism. I will be a supportive, loving wife and mother by leading with grace, kindness, and respect in my home. I commit to my personal standards of excellence, upholding myself to the most superior merit of character and composure at all times.

Your Personal Standards of Excellence must be personal to you, reflecting where your heart truly lies regarding your responsibilities and your willingness to give your best to commitments you cherish.

After you write your Personal Standards of Excellence in your journal, write them on a separate piece of paper and keep them with your Decorum Code, safely tucked in a place that is easy for you to access.

Review your Personal Standards of Excellence once a week by reading them aloud. This will refresh your elegant memory for the upcoming week with the level of excellence you plan to bring to the activities and commitments you made.

* * * * *

ACCOUNTABILITY TO ACHIEVE EXCELLENCE

Hold yourself accountable with your set of personal standards to live a life of excellence. But if you come up short against your personal standards, that never equals failure. Instead of referring to these moments as failures, give yourself grace and regard them as opportunities to learn, grow, and make a change for future improvement. Continuous learning, constant improvement, and a commitment to your personal standards of excellence allow you to tap into your personal power, bestowing upon you the beautiful gift of living your best life.

JE NE SAIS QUOI
Chic Excellence Secrets

- Understand that to live with elegance, you should give your best effort to everything you do.

- Every commitment you make, personal or professional, deserves your full attention, focus, and energy.

- Review your list of current commitments in your journal and reflect on why you are falling short and giving less than your best effort.

- Gracefully step down from opportunities that you are no longer passionate about and for which you give less than your best.

- Strive to operate in the realm of your personal power, where you excel at doing things you love and cherish, helping others along the way.

- Write down your Personal Standards of Excellence and commit to fulfilling them by doing your very best in every role and responsibility you have.

- Read your Personal Standards of Excellence aloud weekly for a quick reminder of how you will navigate your personal and professional responsibilities for the week ahead.

CHAPTER 11

CAREER SUCCESS

I never dreamed about success.
I worked for it.

Estée Lauder

In an ideal world, your career reflects a skill that you both enjoy and are passionate about. In reality, most women find themselves, somewhere along the way, in a career that is unsatisfying or uninspiring. As we explored in the last chapter about your Personal Standard of Excellence, when you lack the passion for what you do, you are also likely to lack the motivation to truly excel.

Passion is the key ingredient to a successful career and a life with je ne sais quoi. When you are passionate about your employment, everyone wins. You win because you have an enjoyable time working. Your clients or customers win because they receive your best work. Your company wins because happy, productive employees are more successful. That success and confidence empower you with elegant satisfaction.

Without passion for what you do in your career, you are essentially trading hours for dollars. Many women find themselves working a job they don't enjoy because of the need for financial support, but that doesn't have to be your reality. Wouldn't it be great to earn money doing something you actually enjoy and not have to endure the mental drain and frustration from an unsuitable employer, boss, or workload?

If you are unhappy in your current career, now is the time for a change. Your lack of passion will affect your work performance (if it hasn't started to already) and be a strong representation of your dissatisfaction. A career change could entail a new job at your current employer, a new employer, or an entirely new industry and career field. The important thing is to find a job doing something that you enjoy. Without genuinely enjoying what you do, you will not be connected to your work or able to achieve career success fully.

You have the limitless opportunity to choose a career that you will love; be happy every morning when you wake up to head to work; and do things you truly enjoy. You can choose to pursue a career that you are passionate about. Or you can choose to be complacent and stay in your job, even if you don't enjoy it, just because it's comfortable. So often in life, we don't choose to pursue our passions and goals; we simply let life happen instead of making it happen. It's time to start making life happen for you! Any professional or career goal you set for yourself is within reach with a plan of action in place to achieve it.

FROM GOALS TO ACHIEVEMENTS

The difference between a goal and a dream is that a goal includes a plan of action to achieve it. Goals are an important part of career success because the accomplishment of an objective is required to be successful. Without a goal, you aren't likely to make an effort or take the initiative to do something ambitious. But with a goal, the outcomes you achieve can surpass your wildest expectations. Goal setting encourages you to leave your comfort zone. Once you accomplish one goal or task, it's time to celebrate the achievement, then plan for the next goal.

Whatever your goals are, whether you want to move to a new city, take up a new hobby, or start a business, a good goal has two parts: an objective and a deadline. What is it you want to accomplish, and when do you want to accomplish it? Both of those answers combined create your goal, and without them, all you have is a dream. But, it's not enough just to create goals. Let's talk about how you can actually achieve them.

There are three secrets of goal setting that can help you to increase your success rate of achievement: writing it down, creating an action plan, and standing on faith.

WRITE IT DOWN

The first secret to goal setting success is to leverage the immense power of written communication. When you have a goal you want to achieve, you should write it down. Writing your goal on paper commits it to your memory. Placing your written goal in a visible location where you can regularly review it reminds you of what you are working toward.

I recommend writing your goal in the present tense as if it has already occurred. This trains your mind to consider it as accomplished already.

For example, instead of writing your goal as: "I will get promoted to Sales Vice President by December of my 40th birthday, and my salary will be $225,000," you can write your goal as: "By December of my 40th birthday: I am the Sales Vice President, and my salary is $225,000."

You will be empowered by writing your goal in the present tense because it feels real and close, within reach.

CREATE YOUR ACTION PLAN

The second secret to goal setting success is to determine your action plan with your to-do list of the steps you need to make it happen. Developing a clear action plan simplifies the process of goal setting to achieve your goals by proactively identifying everything it will take to be successful.

Write down every milestone required to reach your goal, so you have a plan for each step of the journey to accomplishing your goals.

In the example above, I mentioned a Sales Vice President promotion as a potential career goal. The action plan to achieve that goal may look something like this:

1. Take a leadership role on the recently announced company initiative.

2. Present updates on the initiative to my boss and executive team.

3. Document the initiative results.

4. Obtain written feedback and reviews from the team about my input on the initiative.

5. Have a performance review with my manager.

6. Request the promotion.

When you know what it takes to make your goals happen, all you have to do is put your plan into place and carry out each step.

FOCUS YOUR ENERGY ON FAITH

The third and last secret to goal setting success is to fulfill your action plan and rely on the support of faith. When you set a goal, having faith that it is actually possible and that you will achieve it is a vital part of your future success. If you set a goal for yourself and don't think it's within reach, your doubtful mind will share negative thoughts and energy in the universe, influencing your ultimate outcome.

Your energy can either attract or repel your goal. Focus your energy and effort on achieving your goal by fulfilling your action plan, and you will be amazed at what you can accomplish. Visualize your goals already accomplished. Take a few minutes each day to read your written goal aloud then close your eyes and picture it as if it is your current reality. This visualization practice will help you come closer to achieving your goals.

Goals are good to set, but they are only effective when you commit to doing what it takes to achieve success. Your level of commitment and supporting actions determine your future accomplishments.

When you have a high-priority goal that you fully commit to, you can apply relentless perseverance until you achieve it. Spending a few moments (or longer, if needed) each day to focus on your goals, reading them aloud and reviewing your action plans, will be the constant motivational reminder you need for the pursuit of your success.

Actionable Advice

A powerful goal includes an objective and a deadline, written in the present tense.

In your journal, write down your short-term goals (at least five things you want to accomplish in the next one to three years).

Then, write down your long-term goals (at least five things you want to accomplish in the next five to ten years).

Pick one goal to start with, either a short-term or long-term goal, and create an action plan for it. What are all the steps you'll need to take in order to achieve it?

Once your action plan is complete, consider how you can apply faith to your goal. What can you do each day to fortify your mindset and empower yourself to feel as if you've already achieved it?

After you start your action plan for this first goal, take the time to reflect and create action plans for the remaining nine goals in your journal.

*****

VISUALIZE TO MATERIALIZE

Visualization is powerful, and it works. As an elegant woman, you know that in the present you can create your future by picturing yourself doing the activities and having the desires of your heart as if they have already occurred today.

For example, say you want to relocate from Minnesota, USA to London, U.K. in the next four years to pursue a doctoral degree from the London Business School. You can picture yourself waking up in the morning to look outside your window and catch a glimpse of Big Ben, walking to Hyde Park to get some fresh air, and enjoying a spot of afternoon tea at The Wolseley – all before going to class for the day.

A tangible way you can visualize and materialize your goals is to create a vision board and regularly review it. A vision board is a collection of visual elements, pictures, and phrases on a poster or corkboard that represent your goals and the future life you want to have. At the start of each year, you can create a new vision board that accurately reflects your ideal future. By spending a few minutes every day reviewing your vision board, you are reminded of your goals, and by seeing them visually, you can easily picture yourself with the Ph. D. degree, living and loving your new life in London.

NETWORKING TO GROW YOUR CAREER

The single best way to grow your career once you have established the right mindset and goals is to network. A successful career relies on networking to fuel its progression. Career success is never achieved alone. Networking allows you to intentionally connect with people to build professional relationships and share contact information to stay connected.

Talent and skills can take your career far, but networking will take you farther, faster. Who you know, and better yet, who knows you, can lead to job promotions, clients earned, and deals closed.

Wherever you ultimately desire to take your career, networking can support you in getting there. If you want to be an executive at a large company, a leader of a small company, or the owner of your own company, the people you know professionally can set you up for career success. Networking on a regular basis, even when you don't want to move or change career paths, is the smartest way to enjoy the many benefits of networking.

You can successfully network in a variety of ways, both informally and formally.

You never know what good can come from networking when you cross paths with someone new, so it's important to network regularly and often. Attending at least one networking event every week to meet new people in your job function or industry opens up new doors and opportunities for you (and you may even enjoy the social scene while you're at it!).

INFORMAL NETWORKING

Informal networking is casually exchanging career information with the people you happen to cross paths with in everyday life. You can and should network with the people around you in your regular routine because you never know who you can help or who can help you. Opening up to share what you do in your career with acquaintances and strangers you happen to come across gives purpose to chance meetings, like when you meet someone new during a visit to the mall to purchase a new seasonal perfume from Neiman Marcus.

Informal networking is light-hearted and simple. In regular conversations, after making pleasantries, you share what you do in your career with someone in proximity to you, and they do the same. The conversation ends with the exchange of contact information to possibly keep in touch.

Stay ready, so you don't have to get ready.

I believe there are few random occurrences in life. There is a reason to explain almost everything, even if we don't know or understand it. Coincidences are few and far between. Because of the possibility of informally networking anywhere and everywhere, it is best to be prepared.

You can informally network like a savvy socialite by:

- Being prepared at all times to share your professional contact information with anyone you meet.

- Keeping your business cards with you every time you leave home (yes, even in a fast-paced digital world) to share with someone you may connect with on a professional level. If your employer hasn't given you business cards, you can request them by asking your supervisor. If your employer does not provide business cards to employees, or if you are self-employed, you can create your own business cards online for a reasonable price.

- Rehearsing and having an answer to the famous, 'What do you do?' question, so you can avoid making a bad impression from being caught off guard, attempting to respond quickly, and awkwardly sputtering an answer. Whether you are in a new role or have been in your job for a while, practice your response and keep your answer short and sweet.

- Having conversation starter topics for making small talk with someone new. The weather, current events, and hometowns are great topics to keep conversations light and friendly.

Actionable Advice

If you don't own a business card holder, get one.

You can keep this small career success essential in your purse, fully stocked with your cards, so when you reach to hand someone your business card, they are clean, dry, and lipstick-free.

* * * * *

FORMAL NETWORKING

Maintaining your relevance in your career is crucial and is best done by being seen and heard regularly. Networking is critical so that people know you and your skills and can foster a relationship where they like and trust you. People do business with those they know, like, and trust. Consequently, formal networking is one of the most rewarding things you can do for your career's success.

Formal networking, where you attend an event with the intention to network, is more deliberate than informal networking. Whether you visit a job fair, happy hour, or conference, formal networking events are held in a variety of formats and venues. People arrive at a formal networking event with the objective of meeting others to supplement their career in some form or fashion.

Regularly attending networking events will help you to stay active and engaged in your career industry and local community. You may be looking for a new job, interested in connecting with potential clients, or even wanting to make new friends within your career field or industry. Meeting new people who share opportunities or experiences with you is useful and important for career success. Consider networking as a resource to maintain and build your career.

You will become an adept networker the more frequently that you network! Networking often receives a bad reputation and can be intimidating or off-putting, but instead of thinking about it for career conversations exclusively, consider networking as a way to enjoy socializing to make new connections. After meeting a new person at an industry happy hour, if you truly connect, you can always follow up to keep the conversation going and build rapport.

Once you have a good rapport with someone, the professional opportunities are limitless. It only takes one person to make a phone call or an introduction to a colleague for you to see the value of networking.

The benefits of networking often extend beyond just the two people involved, and it quickly has a positive, widespread effect. You can be hired, secure a promotion, or gain a new business client from networking. And you can also help others by introducing them to people you happen to know who can further their career or business as well.

You can formally network like a prominent professional by:

- Asking interesting questions to start or carry a conversation, for example: "Are you a member of this organization?"

- Attending events alone to push yourself beyond your comfort zone and expand your Rolodex. When attending events with friends, you typically avoid mingling with new people because you're having such an enjoyable experience together.

- Eating a meal or snack before attending a networking event, so you don't spit marinara meatballs as you passionately explain your current job role as a Human Resources Director.

- Keeping your business cards in a business card holder in an easy-to-reach pocket in your purse.

- Making eye contact with people when speaking, instead of gluing your eyes to your phone or watch.

- Extending a strong, polished handshake that is web to web, instead of offering your fingers.

- Focusing on connecting. All people have an interesting life story; you just have to get to know them.

- Offering to help others when appropriate. Book and conference recommendations are invaluable to colleagues within your industry.

- Following up with people within 24 hours after meeting that you want to keep in touch with. Send a kind thank you email referencing something from the conversation and request to arrange plans for a future meeting.

- Always using your manners with "Please," "Thank you" and "You're Welcome," when appropriate.

- Attending events with a goal to meet a certain number of people. This sets your intention for your networking experience.

- Dressing appropriately to communicate yourself as a polished professional. The perfect outfit for the bar on Friday night is entirely different from the perfect outfit for networking.

- Allowing other people to speak without interrupting them.

- If you're an introvert, you can thrive at networking events by approaching single people instead of large groups to introduce yourself and start a conversation.

Actionable Advice

Research networking events for your career industry and job field. In your journal, write down four and commit to attending them within the next three months.

Add them to your calendar and purchase tickets or confirm your attendance with an RSVP.

As the events approach, have fun attending them, and make the most of meeting new people!

* * * * *

THE POWER OF A GOOD HANDSHAKE

Have you ever shaken hands with someone that left your hand feeling sore and ready for an ice pack? The lobster claw is one of the worst handshakes (The other is a Dead Fish, where your hand is motionless, without a squeeze or shake).

A handshake is important in every professional environment. You are viewed as confident and powerful when you shake hands with others in a polished way. As an elegant career woman, you can be thoughtful in consistently shaking hands with others in a professional manner.

When you meet someone new, you should stand out of respect and smile as you shake hands. The proper handshake is done standing, never seated. Your body should be positioned squarely to face the person with whom you will shake hands. Your right hand should be extended sideways with your palm facing toward your left side (not down toward the floor). Hands should meet palm to palm (the inside center of your hand) and web to web (the curved area near your thumb).

A polished handshake includes two pumps, up and down before letting go. The grip of the handshake should be firm (not loose and not tight). Lastly, make eye contact, smile, and say a kind phrase during the handshake. For example, say: "It's a pleasure to meet you."

When at work, you should shake hands with both women and men, instead of hugging, and with equal firmness, not a limp grip or an overbearing claw.

THE ROLE OF MENTORS

A mentor is a person who acts as a sounding board and gives you career advice and guidance. Long-term career success is difficult to sustain without a mentor. It is important to not only watch someone seasoned and successful from afar but to also learn directly from them the wisdom and lessons they can impart to you based on their experience. Successful women often cite mentorship as one of the key differentiators that attribute to their prosperous careers.

Everyone should have a career mentor, regardless of age or the level in your career. The best career mentor is someone (either male or female) that has accomplished some of the goals you strive to master in your career.

Thanks to technology, it is now increasingly easier than ever before to find and connect with a career mentor. After identifying a career mentor, either from a mutual friend or colleague, meeting by chance at an event, or browsing a printed publication or social network online, it's best to be direct and make your request for mentorship. Don't allow an excellent mentor to pass you by because you are fearful of asking them for mentorship. Most mentors are flattered and honored to help their mentees, and if you never approach to ask someone to be your mentor, you aren't giving them the opportunity to share their knowledge, wisdom, and expertise.

The most fruitful mentor-mentee relationships are reciprocal. You receive value from your mentor and also give value to your mentor as a mentee. Before approaching a potential mentor, think about what precisely you want from the relationship and exactly what you can provide. Do you want advice on a particular subject or need guidance concerning something specific? Knowing what you hope to achieve from them helps you craft the most appropriate request for their mentorship. What added value can you offer to your mentor? Do you have skills, talents, or time you can contribute to improve their career or life in some way? Be clear on deciding what you can offer to the mentor before requesting mentorship.

As a mentee, you own the relationship. You own the responsibility to manage the calendar and set expectations for what you want from your mentor. All too often, career mentorships fail because the mentee doesn't take the proper initiative. You are the one that needs the mentor. You should organize and plan accordingly. Mentors are invaluable and should be regarded as such. Time is the most precious resource any of us have because we can't obtain more of it; once it is gone, it is gone. Honoring your mentor is best done by respecting their time and attention in the relationship.

Every mentor-mentee relationship is different. Some mentor relationships can include daily or weekly communication via email and monthly or quarterly meetings. Each mentorship experience will be different to fit the needs of the mentor as well as complement their schedule and preference for communication. As a mentee, the highest priority is accommodating the mentor's needs.

Requesting someone to mentor you is best done as an in-person conversation, not over social media, text message, or email. Asking someone to be a mentor is simple and should include you telling the person why you value them and their wisdom, explaining how they could be helpful to you as a mentor, and then finally making the request by asking them: "Would you be open to mentoring me?"

There are various ways you can add value to your mentor, either giving them updates on how the advice they gave you was useful or providing skills to help them. For example, if you are a graphic designer, you could create business flyers or cards for your mentor, free of charge. You should always give back to your mentor in some way.

As a mentee, making the most of the time you have with your mentor is best achieved by having a plan in place. Perhaps you meet once a month for coffee, and you bring questions to ask your mentor. Or you may do lunch once a quarter and have an agenda of discussion topics to review. Regardless of how you structure your mentor-mentee relationship, realize that organization is the key to it thriving and being worthwhile.

THE ROLE OF SPONSORS

Unlike a mentor, a sponsor is a person that acts as an advocate on your behalf when you aren't around, instead of merely coaching you with career advice. An ideal sponsor is at least three to four levels senior to you and can make the difference in your candidacy for promotion or being hired for a job role.

Significant research shows that women are over-mentored and under-sponsored. As such, you should have both a mentor and a sponsor.

Finding a sponsor can be done easily by attending company events and speaking to fellow co-workers or getting involved with various projects that offer more interaction with senior executives. When you find someone that you want to sponsor you (either male or female), you can kindly ask them for a specific amount of time (30 minutes, 45 minutes or 60 minutes) to meet and discuss career or company questions.

Due to the leadership level of a sponsor, being clear with how much time you request and what you want to speak about sets proper expectations with your potential sponsor. It gives them an idea of what you hope to accomplish during the conversation, so they can prepare, if necessary.

As with mentors, sponsors don't carry the relationship—you do. When you request the meeting, you should always set a time on their calendar (with at least one month's notice of time in advance), structure an agenda, share it with them when you confirm the meeting date and time, and bring it with you during your time together. This provides structure to the sponsor relationship. A meeting reminder 24 hours before you are scheduled to meet is helpful in respecting your sponsor's time and other commitments.

Learn from your sponsor how they want to communicate and oblige them. If they prefer phone calls to email conversations, then you should give them a call. If they prefer exchanging emails to setting meetings, then you should send an email. Respecting and honoring your sponsor's preferred method of communication is an integral part of how you manage the relationship.

ACHIEVING WORK-LIFE BALANCE

Work-life balance is possible! The key to work-life balance is that you can have it all, just not all at the same time. As an elegant woman, you know how to manage your time effectively and choose priorities for yourself by balancing the many roles you have in life (mother, wife, employee, daughter, friend, and so on).

Instead of taking on too many commitments that you can't fulfill with your standard of excellence, be selective and commit to things that will not over-extend your energy and mental capacity. For example, understand that by spending an early Saturday morning working, you are missing out on time with family, and that by attending an afternoon movie with family on a Wednesday, you are not using that time to get ahead on an assignment.

True work-life balance is achieved by reviewing the total time in a given period that you divide up and spend across various activities, instead of segments of your time from a given period.

ELEGANT OFFICE BEHAVIOR

Carrying yourself with elegance is not just for navigating social interactions, such as attending informal and formal networking events and meeting with mentors and sponsors. Your sense of elegance should shine throughout your life, at work, home, and beyond. There are a few guiding principles to carrying yourself with elegance at the office so that you can display your competence with classy confidence!

CRYING AT WORK

Under no circumstance should you cry in the middle of the office, unless you just got a phone call with terrible news about a loved one, such as your parents or children. For all other occasions, whether your tears are happy, sad, angry, or upset, they should be shed in privacy, not in public places like hallways, break rooms, lobbies, elevators, or large, open spaces. If you are on the brink of tears and can't hold them in until you reach home at the end of the day, you can go to your car, the restroom, or leave the building.

Upon responding to a question or comment, you may need a few moments to gather yourself before responding appropriately. In that case, you can excuse yourself by saying something like "That's an interesting thought. Let me consider it and get back to you on that." Followed by "Excuse me," before you exit the room (or building, if necessary).

ASSERTIVENESS AT WORK

All too often, women are the last to speak at work. You don't have to ask for permission to share your thoughts and ideas during meetings or brainstorming sessions. Collaboration is only beneficial when everyone has the opportunity to contribute.

You can display elegance at work by actively participating in group projects and meetings with others. Never discount your questions or ideas or thoughts as dumb, unimportant, or even crazy. You have talents, opinions, and creativity that deserve attention. You can thoughtfully think about what you want to say and how you want to phrase things, before speaking; just don't spend so long crafting the perfect sentence that you miss the opportunity to share it!

Instead of waiting for everyone in the room to share their thoughts first, feel free to insert yourself in the conversation. Share your ideas and thoughts during a break or pause in a group discussion or conference call to avoid rudely interrupting or talking over someone.

Be sure to always express your thoughts and ideas in every meeting. Share your unique thoughts, counter or support the comments of others, and, upon speaking up the first time during a meeting or conference call, be sure to contribute throughout the discussion so that you can be an active participant and not just a spectator.

A final rule of thumb for assertiveness is never to be the last person to speak. Contribute early in and throughout the conversation – never wait until the very end to share your perspective.

DEALING WITH RACISM AND SEXISM AT WORK

Racism and sexism at work are illegal and unacceptable, but unfortunately, they do occur. When handling a comment or conversation where someone made a racist remark, the gracious thing to do is to remain calm. Instead of yelling, cursing, screaming, or making a scene, maintain your composure. You may feel like lashing back, but such behavior is not in good taste. Your first line of defense is to take a deep breath and count to ten. If you have trouble maintaining your composure, then it is best to excuse yourself and leave the room or meeting.

If you hear a racist or sexist comment for the first time from someone, you can choose to ignore it and not respond to it directly by changing the conversation topic. Educating people on appropriate workplace behavior is not your responsibility unless you are a human resources professional. You can also choose to address the comment directly by asking: "What did you mean by that?" This allows them the opportunity to explain, clarify, or apologize.

The best course of action to take after hearing racial or sexist comments at work is to explore the policies in place at your organization. This will inform you of the process to file a report after an incident occurs. After filing a report with your firm, always get a copy for your personal records.

If you choose not to file a report with human resources, you can keep your own written records of each incident, including the date, time, people involved, and comments made.

If you choose not to go to human resources to report an incident that occurred only once, I recommend that you go the second or third time with your personal notes of what you experienced in tow.

If comments, jokes, or actions happen so frequently that you can't fulfill your role's responsibilities, then that is considered illegal job discrimination, and you can retain an attorney and handle the matter in a courtroom. It is difficult to prove harassment without tangible evidence, like recorded audio or video, and your personal notes will be considered from your perspective. The matter at hand may become a battle of 'he said, she said.' If you hire legal counsel and go to court, take your copies of filed reports from your human resources department with you to support your case.

If you have been physically or sexually assaulted, then it is best to always immediately report it to human resources and file a police report. You can work with human resources to find a solution to the problem of being around a co-worker or supervisor that physically or sexually assaulted you, whether it's moving your desk or securing a new job in a different department. After being physically or sexually assaulted, you can also hire legal counsel and handle the matter in court.

Crude remarks and jokes about racism or sexism should never be a part of your experience at work. The ultimate power you have is to leave the organization and pursue a new job at a company that values and respects female employees.

Having the courage to speak up immediately when an indiscretion occurs exercises your power to stand up for yourself and maintain your right to a non-discriminatory workplace.

ACHIEVING YOUR CAREER SUCCESS

The real key to career success is to identify the job of your dreams and pursue it. The perfect career is waiting for you; if you aren't currently working in your passion, doing what you love right now. What are you passionate about? You can fulfill your greatness and maximize your personal power by combining the passions in your heart with your talents and skills.

It is easy to feel overwhelmed with pursuing career goals when you have family and financial obligations. However, if you're working at a job you detest and spending the majority of your time exchanging hours for dollars — or if you're happy in your current role but want to reach the next level sooner rather than later – then this is your defining moment to let your chic self truly shine!

You can start to make the necessary changes to achieve career success by creating goals and a plan for your transition and taking action to make your dreams reality. With the motivation and focus to succeed, you can quickly turn your aspirations into actuality.

Chic Career Secrets

- If you aren't happy in your career today, you can always change it by exploring a completely different opportunity or elevating your status to the next level in your current field.

- Write your goals in the present tense, have an action plan for each one, and focus your energy on faith until you achieve them.

- Create a vision board every year and review it weekly to refresh your elegant memory of what you hope to achieve.

- Networking, both informally and formally, connects you to people that can help you get where you want in your career, on the fast track.

- Attend at least four networking events every quarter.

- Identify a mentor and sponsor for advice and support to achieve your career goals.

- Navigate workplace conflicts with composure and confidence by giving intention to your actions and responses in the heat of the moment.

PART 5
COMPOSURE

CHAPTER 12

CAPTIVATING COMMUNICATION

Eloquent speech is not from lip to ear, but rather from heart to heart.

William Jennings Bryan

The ability to foster elegant connections with others is both an art and a skill. Positive connections lead to enriched relationships, which lead to a happier, healthier, more vibrant life. To truly thrive in life, you need to be able to connect with others effectively.

Whether the relationship is professional or platonic, the connection you have with others is always important. As you express your graceful power, you captivate others with your charm, which is an essential element of living elegantly with je ne sais quoi. People are attracted to those they like, which is the process of magnetism, drawing people to you and creating meaningful bonds.

Captivating others is easily achieved with effective communication. Captivating communication is about being attractive during a dialogue exchange, to hold the interest and attention of others. When you captivate others, you are charming and delightful, not dry, boring, emotionless, rude, or curt.

In every conversation with others, regardless of the length, you can be polished, polite, and positive based on the manner in which you communicate. The elegant way to be consistently captivating in conversations is to give intention to your verbal, non-verbal, and written communication with others to always charm and delight them.

A captivating woman is always pleasant and friendly.

Being positive and pleasant at all times is part of an elegant lifestyle. Every captivating encounter should be enjoyable. Upon first embracing a positive lifestyle, you can self-correct your thoughts and actions as needed, and it will become your regular behavior over time. Positivity starts with your mindset because your thoughts control what you say and do, so it's best to keep your elegant mind in check.

Once you commit to thinking positively about all people and situations, you can address every conversation with a pleasant presence. Whether you are at a drug store speaking with a pharmacist, or at dinner enjoying a double date, you should aim to be consistently delightful in your demeanor.

CONFIDENCE AND AUTHENTICITY

Confidence is an element of having captivating interactions with others. Not only do you need to feel good about people and situations to be positive, but you also have to feel good about yourself in order to be authentic. Confident women always command respect and are truly captivating.

For example, upon receiving a compliment on your satin blouse, you can confidently accept it by saying, "Thank you," rather than contradicting the speaker with a phrase to downplay the praise, like, "Oh this old thing? I've had it for ages." A delightful response to a compliment is gracious acceptance, as is offering a compliment in return regarding something you appreciate or enjoy about them.

Your confidence comes from within and ignites your authenticity. You can continuously enhance your confidence and authenticity to be captivating.

Captivating others is not simply a matter of saying pleasant things, essentially telling people what you think they want to hear; it's a matter of being authentic in a positive manner. Words without truth behind them are empty and expressionless. Instead of speaking false statements, speak facts. The adage that honesty is the best policy is a good rule to live by. When you pay someone a counterfeit compliment, they likely know you are being a phony. What you say should always be authentic.

CAPTIVATE WITH TACTFULNESS

To be captivating when you speak, you must think before you speak, especially about *how* you say things. In a conversation, before you speak, consider whether or not what you are about to say is necessary. In conversations, your word choice is just as important as the message you are conveying. We are all guilty of saying things that are best left unsaid. Ask yourself the Elegant Conversation Question before speaking a word or phrase: "Is this the best way to say my idea?"

Consider this scenario: your neighbor, Diane, who cooked dinner for you, asks afterward what you thought of the meal. You want to be honest. So, you say, "It was horrible, that was the worst lasagna I've ever had. The filling was salty, and the pasta was hard." Let's examine this response. Was that the best way to respond to your neighbor? No. By thinking before you speak, and considering *how* you say something, and not just *what* you say, you can be pleasant and polite.

An alternative and far more appropriate response could be, "Diane, I loved the sauce you made from scratch, it was delicious! The meat had a bit more salt than I prefer, though. Next time you make lasagna, want to try my grandmother's favorite recipe together?

I'd love to make it with you!" In this second response, you are honest, kind, and provide a solution with your constructive criticism, and your neighbor will likely appreciate your candor.

CAPTIVATE WITH HUMILITY

Captivating communication also includes a level of humility. During conversations, place attention and interest on the other person to make them feel valued and important. When you care about others, and you show it, you are captivating. You convey you are interested and engaged with someone by considering their feelings before you speak.

Think about a conversation you're not looking forward to having; for example, you have to tell your friend that her favorite cashmere sweater you borrowed has been damaged. Let's add some humility to your conversation to gracefully inform her of your lack of care for her garment. Reflect for a moment. How will the person you are speaking with perceive what you share? If you're concerned your friend will think you carelessly wore the sweater and weren't paying attention, you should say something to address the misperception. Since you've let your friend down, you can acknowledge her disappointment to express compassion and offer a solution. A statement with the humility to admit your mistake and how you will remedy the situation may sound something like this, "Karen, I greatly misjudged how interactive the Morrocan cooking class at Whole Foods would be. I wore your cream cashmere sweater while making Harira Soup last night with Robert, and the tomato stain just won't come out! I've been trying all morning to remove it, without success. I'm so sorry. I just went to St. John and got you a new one, the last sweater they had was your size! And while I was there, I saw this scarf that I thought would pair beautifully with it, so I got that for you, too. I'm sincerely sorry, I learned a lesson this time, and I won't be wearing light-colored cashmere to any more cooking classes!"

You can minimize misunderstandings by asking the Elegant Conversation Question: "Is this the best way to say my idea?" before you speak. Words have power, and you certainly want to use the words you say for good, to keep your relationships thriving.

Humility also lends itself to being intrigued by others. Everyone has interesting habits, hobbies, and lives, and seeing others as just as or more interesting than yourself is always appreciated. When in a conversation with someone new, ask questions, practice mindfulness, and show your enthusiasm. Giving others the opportunity to speak more during a discussion doesn't mean that they dominate; it means that they are delighted. Allow people you speak with to feel like you care about who they are and what they are saying.

ARE YOU HEARING OR LISTENING?

In Chapter 8, Polished Presence, we explored the difference between hearing and listening. Being captivating in a conversation requires both. Hearing the words someone says to you allows you to understand the context of the discussion. Listening to the words someone says to you enables you to process the information so that you can respond with a curious question or insightful reply. People are rarely shown humility, and they will feel energized and come alive upon enjoying a conversation with you.

A captivating encounter with others should occur regularly, not rarely.

STARTING CAPTIVATING CONVERSATIONS

A captivating conversation can be established with a delightful question. Common conversation starter topics include weather, location, occasion, news, traffic, sports, and entertainment. The most common question to ask someone when starting a conversation is, "How are you?"

In general, most people will answer with a canned response of, "fine," or, "good," before asking how you're doing, but you can give more detail in your response to be delightful. You can easily start a conversation with an intriguing answer to the infamous question, "How are you?" An intriguing answer will encourage who you are speaking with to respond with either a statement or question of their own, thus starting a conversation. This technique can be used with new acquaintances, friends, family, or work colleagues.

Here are a few examples of delightful answers to: "How are you?"

- "I'm well. Loving this rainy weather we are having! It's very calming after the last few weeks of hot temperatures we've had."

- "I'm doing well, thank you for asking. Your new office space is gorgeous. It's so bright and energizing! Did you recently re-design it?"

- "I'm well, thank you. It's my first time at this event, do you typically attend every month?"

In the instance that someone doesn't respond with a statement or question, you can ask an additional question using one of the common conversation starter topics to establish a dialogue.

At times, people you encounter will not want to talk much. This could be their temperament, or they could be having a bad day. It happens. In the event that you sense someone doesn't want to be in a conversation because they are giving short answers or responding to you with a dry, expressionless tone, you can end the conversation quickly by telling them it was a pleasure to meet them or it was nice seeing them again. Then take your exit.

BUILDING RAPPORT

The quickest way to build rapport and goodwill with others is to identify similarities between yourself and someone else. If you are meeting someone new, you can easily start a conversation by finding something you both have in common. When asking questions, after someone responds to what you asked, you should give your response before asking an additional question or changing the subject. When either of you experiences the 'Hey, me too!' moment that references what you both have in common, you will likely enjoy discussing that topic, and you should let the conversation continue to evolve.

Polite, pleasant conversations with acquaintances are best facilitated without controversy or conflict. When enjoying small talk with acquaintances and work colleagues, politics, sexual orientation, and religious beliefs should be avoided. Friends and family that you consider loved ones are a part of your inner circle, and thus you can feel comfortable discussing anything with them.

DIFFICULT CONVERSATIONS

In the next chapter, Overcoming Difficulty, we will explore how to handle gracefully negative situations and difficult conversations. Realize that you can still be captivating during times of conflict. Being intentional during tough conversations requires you to consider what you are saying and doing in the moment. Instead of displaying hasty, abrasive behavior, you can maintain your composure and effectively maintain eloquence. A hard conversation can be delivered with a calm tone of voice, facial expression, and thoughtfully selected words.

BODY LANGUAGE

Composure is your ability to be calm and in control of yourself at all times. An elegant woman is always composed. The way you engage others through your body language shows them how you are feeling in the moment.

Your body language, also known as your non-verbal communication, encompasses how you communicate with your eyes, facial expressions, voice, body positioning, and body movements. During an encounter with someone, at any given moment, your body displays how you feel. Body language is important because the subliminal cues express in an evident manner your feelings in the moment, which in turn, influence the other person's feelings. The movements you make with your body are the physical expressions of communication. What you do with your eyes, face, voice, and body during a conversation are telling signs of your emotions, so it is critical that you harness how you are non-verbally communicating with others.

Body language is what you say without speaking.

There are two types of body language: positive body language and negative body language. To be captivating when you communicate, strive always to display positive body language. Positive body language, like when you smile or nod your head, makes you look inviting, friendly, and approachable. Negative body language, like when you frown or cross your arms, makes you look unhappy, upset, and unapproachable.

Captivating others is a matter of being a joy to be around. You can consistently be pleasant in your body language and, therefore, always be captivating.

ELEGANT EYE CONTACT

A lot of what you say with your body language is expressed through your eyes. During a conversation with someone, the best way to maintain positive eye communication is to make eye contact.

When you or someone else is speaking, lock in and look directly into their eyes. This shows them that you are interested in what they are saying and attentive. Being engaged in a conversation is an elegant way to be captivating and makes the person you are speaking with feel like a VIP.

When you look away and avoid eye contact with others as you speak, you display the appearance of being uncertain and lacking confidence. It's acceptable to look away from a person every few seconds when you are speaking in a conversation, and for many people, that is a habit that occurs naturally. But when listening, you should hold the focus on the person speaking and maintain eye contact. As you speak during a conversation, coming back to 'home base' to make eye contact every few moments displays your confidence and certainty in what you are saying.

If you are in a noisy or crowded room, you may be tempted to people watch, but by staying focused on the person you are speaking with, you can effectively display positive body language. Shifty eyes constantly looking around the room when someone is speaking to you makes you look uncomfortable, and it likely makes the person speaking feel uncomfortable, too.

Eyes are the window to your soul.

Your true feelings are often expressed with your eyes. Even without moving your mouth to smile or frown, your eyes express to others how you feel. Contentment and anxiousness are easily conveyed by what your eyes tell others. When you smile, your eyes appear friendly. When you frown, your eyes appear distressed.

When you think about how you appear, you can control how people perceive you, regardless of how you feel. When you are angry or distraught, you can take a few deep breaths to gather your composure and calm yourself down before adjusting your body language. Be mindful that your eyes say to others what you want to tell them.

ELEGANT FACIAL CUES

Emotions are also powerfully conveyed by the expression on your face. What you do with your mouth and nose also displays how you feel to those around you. Happiness, shock, anger, fear, and sadness are expressed by the lines we make in our faces on both the cheeks and forehead.

The best positive facial expression is to maintain a pleasant face with a full or slight smile. During a conversation, smiling makes you look attractive and alluring. Some women are told they look angry just by having a neutral face, without a smile or a frown. If you are perceived as angry, even if you don't feel or act angry, people will think you are angry (remember, perception is reality). So, if people commonly ask you if you are upset or tell you that you look angry, you can make an effort to smile more, showing that you are friendly.

Smiling aimlessly can feel a little silly, especially when you are walking alone—across the room during a shopping trip at Williams-Sonoma, or to and from the subway train—but you can smile faintly by slightly curving the corners of your lips upward instead of fully smiling to show your teeth. Making a habit of smiling not only improves how you appear, but it also improves how you feel, activating positive emotions within yourself and others!

Nodding is another cue to people during a conversation of how you feel in the moment. A gentle nod while listening to someone talk shows that you are paying attention and understand or agree with what they are saying, as if you are responding with, "I know what you mean."

A nod and a smile is the winning combination to be captivating when listening to someone and understanding what they are saying. This makes people feel at ease and comfortable during a conversation.

ELEGANT VOICE PITCH AND VOLUME

Your voice's tone has an incredible impact on sharing how you feel. Voice inflection and volume are indicators that provide context to what you say. Your inflection is the pitch of your voice. Your volume is the degree of the sound of your voice. Vocal tone is one reason why written communication can often be difficult to understand, due to the missing link of context.

Your vocal tone in a conversation tells someone the feelings behind the words that you say, based on the emphasis you give them. Consider how both inflection and volume can make a difference with the way you sound when you speak. For example, the inflection of a question differs greatly from the inflection of a shout.

If a friend asked you if you have seen the newest Broadway show and you answer no, there are several ways that your answer can be interpreted based on your voice's pitch and volume.

- NO! (A high volume and low pitch can be perceived as if you are upset)

- No? (An even volume and high pitch can be perceived as if you are confused)

- no... (A low volume and uneven pitch can be perceived as if you are nervous)

Your tone of voice gives an emotional element to your words, so it's best to use it wisely. The most elegant tone of voice for a captivating presence is an even volume, tone, and pitch.

ELEGANT POSTURE

Posture is an impactful way to both show and feel more positive and powerful, so you can be captivating when you communicate. Your posture is a priority because it shows you are confident when you walk, stand, or sit upright instead of slumping or slouching. Whether you are walking, sitting, or standing, the posture that you have conveys both interest and attention during a conversation. You also appear to be more powerful and in control when you display correct posture alignment. Proper posture also affects your health and mood and is the most comfortable position for your neck, head, chest, and spine. A polished posture reduces tension in your shoulders and neck to make you feel more supported and comfortable.

Good posture can be learned if it is not currently a habit in your lifestyle. By monitoring how you walk, sit, and stand, you can pay attention and make corrections to your body positioning when you notice that you start to slump backward or lean forward.

The ideal posture includes shoulders relaxed down from the ears and back behind your chest. Your head should be up, and your chin should not extend too far forward or backward. Your chest should sit upright. Your spine should be straight and not curved, avoiding either to lean forward or backward.

Polished posture easily becomes a habit the more frequently you do it! Each time you adjust your posture, your body is one step closer to learning how to maintain an elegant sitting or standing appearance.

ELEGANT BODY MOVEMENTS

The manner in which you move or don't move your fingers, hands, and arms shows your level of enthusiasm and mood during a conversation. When you make large movements with your body, you appear out of control, wild and intense. When you stay small and keep your body close together, you appear timid, uncertain and disengaged. Instead of looking like you couldn't care less about the conversation at hand, you want to show your interest and energy in an elegant, not overbearing manner.

Do all good things in moderation. The ideal gestures to display positive body language include smooth, controlled movements. Easygoing movements and gestures display to others that you are energized about the topic at hand and add an appealing nature to your conversations. Pointing to something with your finger is appropriate; however, pointing to someone should always be avoided. Move your hands and arms when you speak to show your enthusiasm for a subject, but keep the movements of your hands and arms within two to three inches on either side of your body to avoid seeming over-stimulated.

WRITTEN COMMUNICATION

Written communication has the most lasting impact on others because it is tangible and carries the longest lifespan. Written words are remembered far longer than spoken words because someone can hold onto written words forever. A card, letter, email, text, or social media post is permanently in the universe once it is created and exchanged. Worthwhile writing conveys your feelings and opinions regarding a subject and is best received when you make it personal to the reader.

KEEPING YOUR WRITING CLASSY

The written word leaves an incredible amount of emotion to be interpreted due to the lack of body language. In order to effectively communicate your emotions, consider how you can thoughtfully express your feelings using words and punctuation. The most captivating written communication you send comes from the heart and genuinely expresses the message you want to convey.

When writing a card, letter, email, or text message, your word choice, spelling, and grammar affect your ability to captivate the recipient. Consider the Elegant Conversation Question: "Is this the best way to say my idea?" not only with verbal communication but with written communication as well. Before writing a phrase, ponder for a moment and reflect by answering the Elegant Conversation Question. The word choices in your written communication should be clear and concise. Does it make sense? Does it get to the point? Does it convey the meaning you intend?

A written message looks hastily prepared with spelling or grammar errors. It makes you appear lazy, rushed, and sloppy when you send someone written communication that doesn't mind proper spelling or grammar. Before sending written communication, one way to easily identify spelling and grammar mistakes is to read it aloud before sending it off. When you read aloud what you have written, you will hear how it sounds and quickly identify any errors you may have missed.

SAVVY SOCIAL MEDIA USE

The topics you share on social media should be thoughtfully chosen. Social media is a public arena to share information; thus, it is essential to be careful, giving thought to the information you share online. It is not the most captivating form of communication, but it is the most widespread way to communicate because you are one person broadcasting a message to many people. Social media is a permanent form of communication that is not deleted and never dissolves in thin air. Anything shared online lasts forever. As an elegant woman, it's important to be intentional and think about what you share before posting on social media platforms, either on your own page or commenting on another person's page.

Social media is not the best form of communication by which to have a meaningful connection with someone. Social media is a difficult way to communicate because it cannot include sparkles of non-verbal communication (your eye contact, facial expressions, body movements, and tone of voice). Therefore, it can be difficult for others to understand the context of what you meant in a social media post. Worthwhile, meaningful connections are best facilitated in person.

Because of the level of high transparency that social media has, it is best to avoid sharing your personal opinions on the same topics that should be avoided in small talk conversations: politics, sexual orientation, and religious beliefs. The privacy settings of your accounts do not protect your posts from being shared with mixed company. It only takes one click of a button to grab a screen image of your social media profile.

It is best to err on the side of caution when sharing things on social media. Sharing what your individual beliefs are is appropriate and acceptable because that is a part of your being. Sharing what your *opinions* are is not appropriate or acceptable. You may want to discuss the matters with friends and family; however, keep those conversations offline to minimize the risk of your private conversations becoming public.

As an elegant woman, you hold yourself to a certain standard and would never want to be portrayed negatively. In order to not misrepresent yourself, it's best to think twice before posting any image, text, or comment on a social media platform. The one guiding social media principle is to consider if you would be proud should what you posted end up on the front page of your local newspaper.

When you have urgent or important information to share—such as learning you are pregnant, earning a promotion at work, or getting engaged—social media should not be the first place that you go to express it to close friends and family. Acquaintances can learn of the news on social media, but your loved ones should not have to read about it online first. A common courtesy is to share important news with loved ones verbally, either in person or over the phone, before you post it on social media. By using common sense and thinking courtesy first, you can be captivating both online and offline.

MAINTAINING YOUR CAPTIVATING CHARM

Communication is a beautiful way to express your thoughts and emotions and should be done with taste in order to captivate and delight others. Thoughtful intention should always be given to what and how you speak, walk, sit, stand, and write.

The key to being captivating when you communicate is to make courtesy a top priority. What you communicate and share with others, whether verbal, physical or written, should include a touch of humility and consider the other person or people involved. Your politeness toward others shows them that you care about them and their feelings, which conveys your elegance. When you think before you communicate, you can be sure that you are captivating in every encounter.

Chic Communication Secrets

- Every time you communicate with others, whether it's an acquaintance, colleague, friend, or family member, strive to be elegant and eloquent.

- Before you speak, ask yourself the Elegant Communication Question, "Is this the best way to say my idea?"

- To exercise humility and gracefulness, consider how your message will be perceived before you speak.

- Mind your eye contact, facial expressions, body movements, and tone of voice to be intentionally elegant in every interaction.

- Before posting anything on social media, reflect on whether or not that post would make you proud if you saw it on the front page of your local newspaper.

CHAPTER 13

OVERCOMING DIFFICULTY

I can be changed by what happens to me, but I refuse to be reduced by it.

Dr. Maya Angelou

Composure is easy to maintain in a pleasant, casual, or relaxed environment, but in times of difficulty, it will be a test for you to stay calm under pressure. When someone is rude during a disagreement or the mood is hostile, remaining composed is not always easy, but it is always possible. As we reviewed in the last chapter, Captivating Communication, composure is your ability to be calm and in control of yourself at all times. This is the divine power of choice, an option always available to you. In the heat of a conflict, you can choose to argue, shout, and curse, or you can choose to remain quiet, be kind, or apologize.

When you fail to retain your composure—like becoming infuriated, cursing, and screaming at Saks Fifth Avenue because you can't return a green Oscar de la Renta evening gown you purchased on clearance—you are acting carelessly, flying off the handle and treating others with disrespect. It is never acceptable to treat people disrespectfully, even if you are being disrespected yourself. Difficult situations give you the opportunity to elegantly display your composure, your ability to retain your graceful demeanor of calm, cool, and collectedness despite the circumstance.

You can practice problem-solving by taking deep breaths and thinking before speaking, acting, or reacting in a situation when there is conflict. For example, when in a conversation with a travel agent, and you've just been insulted because of your lack of knowledge about Europe, you can take a deep breath and think before speaking or reacting. This gives you a chance to be intentional and give a polite response, then excuse yourself from the toxic conversation and leave the building.

Even with minor infractions that are inconvenient throughout your day, like when your waiter at Nick and Sam's brings you a steak when you ordered trout for dinner, you can take a deep breath and think before speaking. By being kind yet firm and honest with the waiter, you're more likely to enjoy the rest of your dining experience.

You have the beautiful opportunity to practice composure when difficulties arise. When you carry yourself with elegance and composure, you choose not to carry the burden of acting upset and flustered during conflict situations. The source of the conflict or difficult situation never impacts your composure. Composure is a choice to display poise, not hostility.

When you carry yourself gracefully with composure, whether or not the recipient has earned or deserves your kindness is irrelevant. The elegant woman you are knows to always treat others with courtesy and respect, the way they *should* be treated, not the way they always treat you or the way you think they *deserve* to be treated.

MANAGING YOUR EMOTIONS

When you manage your emotions first and then respond, you give yourself time to react from the inside out, instead of from the outside in. The Elegant Inside-Out Technique is when you manage how you feel internally before you control what you do externally. There's also the Elegant Outside-In Technique when you first manage what you do with your reaction and the words you say before addressing your internal emotions.

Notice the important word in these empowering, elegant actions is "manage." You can't control your emotions. When you are mad, you feel mad. When you are frustrated, you feel frustrated. What you can do is *manage* your feelings. When you manage an emotion, you take account of what that emotion is and how you feel. Then you can re-position yourself with elegance, thinking about positive thoughts and finding the silver lining by asking the Elegant Mindset Question: "What is the good in this situation?" Re-position yourself with elegance to improve how you feel after a challenging experience or situation.

An example of the Elegant Inside-Out Technique is arriving at the spa with your two best friends for a weekend getaway. One of your friends scheduled the appointment for the three of you several months ago, in April. While speaking to the concierge, you learn that the scheduled appointment date has come and gone, and the spa is fully booked for the remainder of the year! Your friend who called to book your spa retreat weekend was given the correct dates of the month (the 3rd – 6th), but the incorrect month (May instead of June). The three of you have cleared your work calendars for this weekend and have been anticipating it for months. You take a deep breath and ask yourself the Elegant Mindset Question: "What is the good in this situation?" Within a few moments, you recall that you have 40,000 hotel points that expire in two weeks, so you enthusiastically share with your friends how you three can make the best of this girls' getaway weekend, complete with a complimentary hotel suite and daily room service!

In most cases, the Elegant Inside-Out Technique is the most effective. However (because everyone is different), if you find that by thinking elegantly first before acting isn't helpful, try managing your body language and actions first to influence more positive emotions and thoughts. In the middle of a difficult situation, smile, nod your head, make eye contact, and maintain a relaxed tone of voice, even if you don't feel like it. All you may want to do is scream and curse, but that is neither exercising composure nor acting in good taste. Instead, display a graceful, poised presence, and it will help you to feel more at ease and be perceived as more relaxed, too.

GIVING INTENTION TO YOUR THOUGHTS

Overcoming difficult situations all starts with your mindset. Your ability to maintain composure during conflict relies on the foundation of consistently having positive thoughts. In Chapter 1, Mastering Your Mindset, we explored the impact that your thoughts have on every area of your life. Your perspective of a situation shapes how you act and react. Remember your two inner critics, the positive and negative consciences? You can listen to either conscience as the inner voice that guides your thoughts. During a difficult situation, having a strong mindset, brimming with optimism, helps you find hope in times of despair. Practicing a life of optimism helps you to embrace each day with positivity, so you can successfully navigate difficult situations with composure and dignity.

Life happens. Sometimes how you feel can affect your mood, like if what someone said or did to you leaves you feeling irritated and upset. When you have a day that you wish had gone better, instead of lashing out at someone with anger or frustration, you can maintain your composure by staying calm, cool, and collected. The negative emotions you feel don't need to be broadcasted or shared. On days that you feel upset, stressed, or annoyed, instead of conveying the negativity to others (misery loves company!), you can simply shake it off.

Any day when you don't feel your best is not a bad day unless you choose for it to be a bad day. You can choose to find joy and create happiness in dark, troubling times. When unfavorable circumstances occur, you have the choice to react and deal with the situation on your own elegant terms. What you choose to focus on and think about fuels your emotions. To manage your emotions, you must first control your thoughts. When a difficulty occurs, you can replace negative thoughts with contentment and gratitude, improving how you physically feel with vibrant, positive emotions.

It may not be easy to always look on the bright side, but with repetition, it will become an easier and more routine part of your life. When you modify how you think about a person or situation, you can adjust your behavior, so that what you say or do is classy and composed.

THE ELEGANT RESET

When faced with a trying situation, you can do what I like to call an Elegant Reset. The Elegant Reset is a collection of actions you can use to physically release any tension and stress you are carrying at the moment. An Elegant Reset starts with eyes closed to relax your mind. As you inhale through your nose, you release the negative emotions, and as you exhale, sighing aloud, ask yourself the Elegant Mindset Question: "What is the good in this situation?" This will help you find the silver lining in the situation.

MANAGING STRESS

Stress is usually physically felt within your body in your neck, stomach, back, shoulders, or even with a headache. Different women feel stress in different places. When your muscles tighten, you experience stiffness or aching pain, your stomach feels like it's in knots, or you feel dizzy or light-headed, that is a sign you are carrying stress, which is a much heavier load to carry than a Longchamp tote filled with your laptop and daily cosmetics.

We often carry tension in our bodies, adding to the burden of feeling stressed.

To avoid stress, manage your emotions by reflecting on gratitude for the good things you have in your life, and you will physically start to feel better. Regular relaxation also helps you reduce stress as well as talking to a friend or loved one who will lend a listening ear. Physical activities, including running, walking, dancing, biking, hiking, swimming, or kickboxing minimize stress and are great confidence boosters, too! You can also avoid caffeine, alcohol, and nicotine to mitigate or prevent stress.

Self-care is vital for your health, to relax, recharge, and minimize stress. An elegant life is full of peace and joy, not stress and frustration. Being intentional with how you choose to respond and what you do to maintain your elegant composure makes a world of difference in your life with je ne sais quoi.

Actionable Advice

The next time you are stressed, try a new approach to relieve your tension and anxiety, whether it's talking to a loved one, practicing an Elegant Reset, or focusing on optimistic thoughts.

You will begin to notice the difference as you sprinkle composure and grace on your mindset and actions, instead of continuing to feel flustered and upset.

* * * * *

THERAPY THROUGH MUSIC

Music is therapy for your soul. When you listen to a song, it can move you in a powerful way. When listening to music, you can feel more confident and vibrant, ready to take on the world, or sullen and stuck in misery, wanting to play the victim. Different songs have different impacts on your feelings. For example, blues music can make you feel like getting over your ex-boyfriend will be near impossible, but pop rock music can make you feel empowered, like a conqueror, like this breakup was closing one door to open a better one!

Actionable Advice

Depending on the song you play, you can feel inspired, beautiful, happy, reflective, sad, lonely, or broken. An elegant life is always about positivity, not negativity.

Create your Je Ne Sais Quoi Soundtrack, a collection of songs that inspires and motivates you to feel your very best!

You can include as few or as many songs as you like!

Write your list of songs for your Je Ne Sais Quoi Soundtrack in your journal. Then, make the playlist on your platform of choice so you can play it whenever you may need to elevate your day or mindset with elegance.

Use the power of music to encourage you to live each day with elegance, especially when difficulties or challenges arise.

* * * * *

GRACEFULNESS WITH GRATITUDE

If you have a day when you don't feel your best, an Elegant Reset eases your body, mind, and soul. An Elegant Reset combined with focusing on gratitude can turn around your entire day, week, month, or year. Instead of focusing on what is going *wrong* in your family, marriage, friendships, or career, focus on what is going *right*. You woke up today, and that is an incredible reason to be grateful. As you do a set of Elegant Resets, mentally make a list of everything that you are grateful for in your life today. Your health, family relationships, friendships, past accomplishments, talents, and passions are all wonderful sources of gratitude.

An attitude of gratitude helps you find joy during difficulty.

RESPONDING TO RUDENESS

As a woman of composure, you set the standards and examples for others to follow. In some situations, people will aggravate you, hoping to get a reaction. Those are the times when you should make your best effort to maintain composure. The ability to stay graceful during a negative situation is the ultimate display of your elegance. That is your shining moment to display character and poise, to be true to who you are as a woman with je ne sais quoi. There is no need to treat others the way you are treated. You treat others the way you know you should treat them – with respect, kindness, and courtesy – at all times.

On any given day, you could come across someone who is having a day when they feel less than their best. Unless someone tells you precisely what is wrong with them, you never truly know what someone is going through. A person could be experiencing a recent death in the family, dealing with a financial issue, or having trouble in their marriage. Regardless of why someone is troubled, you owe them grace. The ability to show compassion to someone despite their lack of kindness toward you is the true testament of composure.

OVERCOMING DIFFICULTY

When people are rude, the best response is to rise above the rudeness.

Rudeness can arise from others when you least expect it. The first thing to consider when someone is rude to you is not to take it personally. You may not necessarily know what troubles someone, but you can take comfort in the fact that it is not about you.

When you take things personally, you overburden yourself without good reason. Consider how trivial the matter is instead of getting upset. For example, when preparing to pull into a parking spot at Bergdorf Goodman, and someone cuts you off to take the spot you were waiting on, think first, "Is this situation really worth getting upset?" Never let anyone have the power to steal your joy. Keep your cheerful spirit at all times. The most appropriate response to rudeness is to do an Elegant Reset and be light-hearted in your response. Kind words, a calm tone of voice, and a pleasant presence do wonders for both you and the person being rude to you. You may even help inspire them to have a much more positive day after interacting with you once you show them such incredible kindness.

HANDLING CRITICISM

Everyone has an opinion, but not every opinion needs to be shared. In the event that someone feels strongly enough to share their opinion with you, you can take heart in the fact that they felt both comfortable and compelled to give their two cents. Never get defensive. Upon hearing criticism from someone, the best course of action to take is separating the constructive from the destructive feedback. Constructive criticism exists to inspire improvement and development in others. Destructive criticism exists to nitpick, provoke, and anger others. The main difference between the two is that constructive criticism is shared for the person hearing the feedback and destructive criticism is shared for the person giving the feedback (perhaps they just want to 'get something off their chest').

When you receive criticism and before responding, first determine if it's constructive or destructive. Will this improve or help you in some way or is it just an opinion that finds fault about something you said, did, or wore? The appropriate response to criticism is to thank the person that shared their thoughts with you. Saying, "Thank you for letting me know," is always appropriate. If the criticism is constructive, you can choose to consider it as advice for the future, and that is entirely up to you. You aren't obligated to take the feedback of others to heart; you have the choice to do so. If the criticism is destructive, you should let it go in one ear and out the other.

Most opinions that people have are best kept to themselves.

This is true for others, and it is also true for yourself. We are all blessed with varying perspectives, ideas, and thoughts. Because everyone has free will to live their lives in a manner of their choosing, their actions, presence, and wardrobe are entirely up to them to individually decide. When you see someone and happen to disagree with something they said, did, or wore, it is not your place to share that feedback unless the person asks for it. Unsolicited feedback is the worst kind.

The main exception to the 'no feedback' rule is in your career. As a manager or supervisor, you are in a leadership role, and providing guidance and direction is one of many job requirements. In that case, giving constructive criticism is ideal for you to help influence your team members to improve their personal and professional lives. The delivery of constructive criticism should always be done tastefully in a calm, reassuring way to support and encourage improvement from your colleagues.

ELEGANT APOLOGIES

In an imperfect world, we are imperfect people, which means that we will all make mistakes from time to time. When you make a mistake, you must own up to it to navigate the difficult situation with elegance. When you are in the wrong, there is no harm in taking ownership not only to recognize that fact but also to acknowledge it. When appropriate, a sincere apology should be made instead of avoiding addressing the issue with others. A sincere apology includes the heartfelt words, "I'm sorry," along with recognition of what the mistake was and a genuine commitment to avoid making it again. There is no need to dwell on the mistake that either you or someone else made. After a conversation has addressed the issue, you should move past the conflict without continuously needing to bring it up or discuss it.

HAVING DIFFICULT CONVERSATIONS

Having a difficult conversation with someone is never an enjoyable experience, but you can make the most of it by mastering the art of your elegant composure. If you have to share bad news with someone or happen to have a differing opinion with them on a particular subject, present yourself elegantly to make the moment manageable. Positive body language plays a large role in elegantly approaching difficult conversations. An even tone of voice, relaxed facial expression, and proper posture help you to feel and look more composed in the heat of the moment.

When discussing a difficult matter, your word choices should be direct and straightforward. Instead of avoiding the issue at hand, be clear and upfront by sharing the facts (not your opinion) regarding the matter. A difficult conversation is the worst time for humor but the best time for empathy. You may not smile when sharing bad news or expressing disagreement, but you can maintain a pleasant presence with positive body language. This is not easy. The easy way out is to say exactly what you are thinking and completely disregard the feelings of the other person involved. Exercising composure during difficult conversations gets easier the more frequently you exercise courage for composure.

Honesty is the best policy. Always. Being truthful in what you say and considering the Elegant Conversation Question: "Is this the best way to say my idea?" will guide you to be polite during a difficult conversation. And it should be just that: a conversation. Don't dominate by doing all the talking. It is essential when sharing bad news or expressing disagreement that both people can voice their concerns. When the other person or other people are talking, actively listen to hear what they say instead of speaking over them or preparing your next thought.

Your opinions and advice are best omitted from difficult conversations. If someone asks you for advice or your opinion, only then is it appropriate to share it. In such a conversation, you should focus on the facts to avoid portraying people or situations in a melodramatic light. Before you speak with someone in a difficult conversation, consider how you would feel if being told the same information. By making the other person and their feelings a priority, you can be more courteous in your approach to the conversation. Difficult conversations may not be fun to have, but you will likely face them throughout life. Your ability to set the tone for the conversation with composure can help ease the burden and challenge of having a difficult conversation.

LET COMPOSURE LEAD

Composure is often tested during challenging situations, but you can successfully maintain it by being thoughtful and careful when you face a conflict. Your ability to manage your emotions helps you to control your thoughts, and thus, control your actions. An elegant life with je ne sais quoi is led with composure, even in the most challenging of times. We can't control many situations in life, but what we can control is how we respond and react. Always remember that your actions show someone who you are while your words only tell them. What you do during difficult situations displays the true testament of who you are. Your character is the foundation of your guiding principles, and it has the opportunity to shine in times of conflict or chaos. Ultimately, you have the power and control to always share the best, most elegant version of yourself with the world.

Chic Composure Secrets

- You have total control and power over your mind, words, and actions. Be intentional in what you think, say, and do during difficult situations.

- In a difficult situation, use the Elegant Inside-Out Technique to sprinkle positivity in your mind before speaking.

- In a difficult situation, use the Elegant Outside-In Technique to be polished in your words and body language, leading to more positive thoughts.

- After a conflict occurs, ask yourself the Elegant Mindset Question: "What is the good in this situation?"

- When you are at your tipping point, before losing your temper, do an Elegant Reset to calm your mind and body, relieving stress and re-positioning your mind with positivity.

- Create your Je Ne Sais Quoi Soundtrack with amazing, uplifting songs and play the music whenever you want to add a dash of elegance to your day!

- Be intentional to treat others with grace, whether or not you think they deserve it.

- Always remember that your actions show someone who you are, while your words only tell them.

CHAPTER 14

EVERYDAY ELEGANCE

Elegance is when the inside is as beautiful as the outside.

Coco Chanel

The essence of living an elegant life is to carry yourself with poise, composure, dignity, and grace. Elegance is a refined way of living that is reflected in how you think, walk, talk, act, and dress. When present, it can and does influence everything you do. When elegance is something you routinely exhibit, you enjoy a life with je ne sais quoi. It becomes a part of you as a woman, not just an occasional occurrence.

You may be wondering how to fill your life with days of elegance. An elegant lifestyle is achieved by being thoughtful and carefully bringing intention to everything you do: how you think, how you look, and how you live. The decisions you make for how you live every element of your life ultimately create your lifestyle.

Appearance is often the first thing that comes to mind upon the mention of elegance. While style and personal grooming are elements of being elegant, they are not the *only* elements that define elegance. Elegant living is a lifestyle. Everyday elegance refers to living your life in a tasteful manner. As such, cultured thoughts and actions, combined with a chic appearance, lead to a life with elegance.

HOW TO THINK ELEGANTLY

An elegant woman is a confident woman. Confidence is at the core of both elegance and je ne sais quoi, which is why that is the first section of this book. When you are self-assured and certain within yourself, you are confident. When you are confident and not arrogant, you are elegant. Knowing your value and your worth empowers you to be firm in who you are as a woman, mother, wife, and friend. Confidence is exuded in elegance.

Elegant thoughts always include optimism. When you spend time listening to your positive conscience and focus on positive things, you will interact with others in a cheerful, pleasant manner. You've likely heard the phrase before: you get out what you put in. This alludes to the fact that you will only be able to act and do things based on what you are constantly thinking. Think about good things, and you will have good days and create a good life.

Gratitude is the most tangible way to start training your mind to be elegant and optimistic. This is why Gratitude Journaling is a powerful way to spend each morning for some 'me time' of reflection. When you spend time counting your blessings and realize just how much you have to be thankful for, you will be more in tune with positive, pleasant thoughts and therefore be more positive and pleasant with others.

Cultivating elegant thoughts may be easier said than done, but once you begin to complete, review, and apply the exercises from this book, you will find that you can re-train your mind to think with elegance. Always focus on the good in people, places, and things. When in a difficult situation, ask yourself the Elegant Mindset Question: "What is the good in this situation?"

You can find the silver lining in any situation under the sun—you just have to look for it.

HOW TO LOOK ELEGANT

Despite trendy fashions of revealing, skin-tight clothing aiming to expose as much of your body as possible, that does not create an elegant appearance. An elegant appearance takes into account being respectful of others and respectful of yourself.

Respecting others refers to wearing attire appropriate for every occasion. For example, you likely wouldn't wear dirty, paint-stained clothes on a dinner date at the Ritz-Carlton; instead, you likely would signify the occasion by wearing something clean, dressy, and polished. Respecting yourself refers to keeping areas of your body covered that do not need to be on public display, namely your midriff, bosom, and derrière.

A chic appearance leaves something to the imagination. Tasteful clothes don't have to be baggy, archaic, or gloomy, making you look like an old maid. Tasteful clothes simply cover the three areas of your body that you should want to keep to yourself, as previously listed.

An elegant appearance is always polished and pulled together. Despite your Elegant Style Personality, you can have an elegant appearance by minding the details of what you wear and how you maintain your personal grooming. An elegant appearance is not about wearing dresses and heels, but about being tasteful and well-kept.

To achieve an elegant appearance, you must be thoughtful to plan and prepare your wardrobe for each occasion. As you manage your social calendar and dress for various events and activities, be mindful of the dress code. It could be either formally established, like a cocktail party invitation with a 'cocktail attire' dress code, or informally assumed, like a professional networking event hosted by your local association, where you will wear business casual. With or without a dress code, it is presumed that most adults know how to present themselves appropriately and will do so accordingly. In the case that no dress code is included on the invitation for an event you are attending, it is best to err on the side of being overdressed rather than underdressed.

The manner in which you prioritize personal grooming will be the final polishing touches on your elegant appearance. Well-kept hair, nails, teeth, and skin radiate when they are healthy. Regardless of your beauty preferences—short or long hair, polished or unpolished nails—the overall impression that elegance gives off is apparent when your look is consistently neat and tidy. Everyday elegance requires regular self-care and proper maintenance, as we previously explored in Chapter Five, Beauty Routine, and Chapter Six, Healthy Habits. When you make your appearance a priority, not only do you reap the benefit of extra confidence, but you command power, prestige, and respect from people around you.

HOW TO LIVE ELEGANTLY

Elegant living is an art form that people are delighted to experience due to its rarity. It's no secret that most women are not elegant. When you treat others with respect, courtesy, and kindness, you are leaving a memorable, lasting impression that is sure to be cherished. Being thought of as elegant and sophisticated is one of the greatest compliments someone can pay you.

An elegant life is a higher form of living compared to an average life. When you feel and look your best, you will live your best life. Each day is a special gift to appreciate and enjoy. Living with elegance empowers you to fill the days, weeks, and months in a year with joy, positivity, happiness, and beauty. There is nothing better than living with elegance!

The simple golden rule, to treat others the way you want to be treated, is at the heart of living with elegance. Always remember the famous quote by Dr. Maya Angelou: "People will forget what you said, people will forget what you did, but people will never forget how you made them feel." How you treat others is what ultimately confirms or denies your elegant life. The most impeccably dressed woman with a foul mouth and horrible attitude is not elegant; she is merely well-dressed. As you think elegant, positive thoughts, you will, in turn, be positive in your actions and treat others with courtesy and kindness.

Elegant actions are based on a simple concept: courtesy first. When you ask a cashier at Burberry what time the store closes, be courteous. When you answer the hostess's question over the phone about how many people you'd like to make a reservation for at Ruth's Chris, be courteous. When sending an email to your mother with a list of potential destinations for your family's upcoming cruise, be courteous. Applying courtesy to every question, answer, email, and phrase that you speak is how you can live elegantly.

Adding a dash of kindness to your actions occurs only when you intentionally think before doing or saying something. As we explored in previous chapters, there are graceful ways to treat people in what you do and say so that your actions are aligned with your intentions of being elegant.

An elegant life is a life with je ne sais quoi. When you are careful to select your thoughts, wardrobe, and actions with intention, you can ensure that you are elegant at all times. Elegance has a magnetizing effect on others that allows you to have enhanced self-awareness, stronger relationships, and an overall higher quality of life.

Chic Everyday Secrets

- Focus on positive thoughts to apply optimism to every area of your life. Your most consistent thoughts motivate what you say and do when interacting with others.

- Always look for the silver lining in a difficult situation by asking yourself the Elegant Mindset Question: "What is the good in this situation?"

- Respect others by dressing appropriately for every occasion, whether it has a dress code that is formally expressed or informally assumed.

- Respect yourself by keeping your midriff, bosom, and derrière covered.

- Remember and apply the golden rule to always treat others the way you want to be treated.

- In everything you say and do, think courtesy first to always lead with kindness.

- Live with intention by carefully considering what you say, do, and wear to always live with elegance.

The Journey of Je Ne Sais Quoi

Nothing can dim the light that shines from within.

Dr. Maya Angelou

You may be wondering what's next. I hope that this book has inspired you to strengthen your mindset, discover your true self, refine your style, upgrade your self-care, improve your presence, increase your career success, and enhance your life. You have now created your alluring sense of je ne sais quoi, your Elegant It-Factor, which will empower you to be captivating, graceful, and refined every day. The truth of the matter is that this is only the beginning. You will develop and evolve as you experience life. Goals will be set, accomplishments will be made, and fears will be conquered.

It was my pleasure to write this book for you, guiding you on the journey of adding je ne sais quoi to your life. I hope that after reading it, you are a better woman, mother, wife, friend, and colleague. I have one final challenge for you: harness the power of being the best version of yourself and live with elegant intention every day for the rest of your life. Being a phenomenal woman shouldn't be applied exclusively to your favorite social events or with your closest friends. Being a phenomenal woman is who you are. It's the essence of your character.

At the dawn of every new year, as you celebrate the exciting, fresh start of your next chapter in life, I encourage you to review and take an audit of yourself and your lifestyle. Who do you want to be? What are your goals? What has changed from the last year and what has remained the same? A life with je ne sais quoi is about bringing intention to what you think, say, do, and wear so that you can always be elegant and captivating. When you decide who you want to be and how you want to live, you can maintain your character in every situation that comes your way, good or bad, easy or difficult, positive or negative.

To be an inspiring, positive, encouraging woman in this world of darkness is not only an honor but your way of giving hope to others. Your joy radiates in a world full of negativity, depression, sadness, and turmoil. Never dim your light. We need you, now more than ever. So, keep trailblazing, keep shining, and keep your heels, head, and standards high.

Acknowledgments

First and foremost, thank you to God and my Lord and Savior, Jesus Christ, for arming me with the courage and conviction to embrace a life of elegance – and giving me the words to show others the way. Without You, none of this would be possible, and I am grateful.

Thank you to my family, who encouraged me to never give up on my dreams of writing this book and always shared an inspirational word when I needed one.

Thank you to my daughter Nyla, who relentlessly supports me and patiently sacrificed what seemed like 'forever' as I wrote, edited, revised, and re-read version upon version of this masterpiece until it was complete.

Thank you to Jennifer L. Scott for being an inspiration to countless women around the world to live a chic life with polished poise. I greatly appreciate your support of this book, and am so delighted you contributed the foreword.

Thank you to the immense group of people that helped me throughout the process of planning, researching, writing, editing, refining, designing and promoting this book, namely Tonda Nelson, Lori Arnold, Jacqueline Baker, Jessica Parker, Daymond Lavine, Cynthia Childress and Susannah Russell.

And last but certainly not least, thank you to every woman who reads, learns and applies what is in this book. I appreciate your kind patronage and wish you much success, love and happiness.

About the Author

Devoreaux Walton is an author, speaker and online personality who serves as the CEO and Founder at The Modern Lady, a lifestyle company that educates and empowers women to confidently live their best lives. Devoreaux shares her knowledge of mindset, personal style, etiquette and communication skills with women to help unlock the lady within and harness their feminine power.

Devoreaux brings to her clients over ten years of experience styling and inspiring women around the world. After graduating from Spelman College with a Bachelor of Arts in Psychology, and Washington University in St. Louis with a Master of Business Administration with a Marketing Concentration, she began her career in the world of marketing. She brings corporate experience from Google, IBM and several start-up organizations to help women elevate both their personal and professional lives.

Devoreaux has worked with senior executives, political candidates and fashion shows. Over the years, Devoreaux has been featured in many publications, including *Forbes*, *Cosmopolitan*, *Brides Magazine*, *Authority Magazine*, and *Apartment Therapy*.

Learn more at
www.DevoreauxWalton.com

PART 6
CLASS